# Spelling Skills

## Grade 3

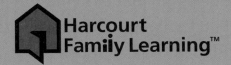

## Harcourt Family Learning™

FLASH KIDS and the distinctive Flash Kids logo are registered trademarks of Barnes & Noble Booksellers, Inc.
Harcourt Family Learning and Design is a trademark of Harcourt, Inc.

© 2005 Flash Kids
Adapted from *Steck-Vaughn Spelling: Linking Words to Meaning, Level 3*
by John R. Pescosolido
© 2002 Harcourt Achieve
Licensed under special arrangement with Harcourt Achieve.

For more information, please visit flashkids.com
Please submit all inquiries to Flashkids@sterlingpublishing.com

ISBN 978-1-4114-0384-0

Manufactured in China

Lot #:
28  30  29
06/20

FlashKids

New York

# Dear Parent,

As your child learns to read and write, he or she is bound to discover that the English language contains very many words, and that no single set of rules is used to spell all of these words. This can feel rather confusing and overwhelming for a young reader. But by completing the fun, straightforward activities in this workbook, your child will practice spelling the words that he or she is most likely to encounter in both classroom and everyday reading. To make the path to proper spelling even easier, each lesson presents third-grade words in lists grouped by vowel sound, suffix, or related forms, like plurals and contractions. This order will clearly show your child the different ways that similar sounds can be spelled.

Each of the 30 lessons begins by asking your child to say each word in the word list. This exercise helps him or her to make the connection between a word's appearance and what it sounds like. Next, he or she will sort the words, which teaches the relationship between a sound and its spelling patterns. Your child will then encounter a variety of activities that will strengthen his or her understanding of the meaning and use of each word. These include recognizing definitions, synonyms, and base words, as well as using capitalization and punctuation. Be sure to have a children's or adult dictionary available, which your child will need to use for some of the exercises. Each lesson also features a short passage containing spelling and grammar mistakes that your child will proofread and correct, using the proofreading marks on page 7. Once he or she can recognize both correct and incorrect spellings, your child is ready for the next lesson!

Throughout this workbook are brief unit reviews to help reinforce knowledge of the words that have been learned in the lessons. Your child can use the answer key to check his or her work in the lessons and reviews. Also, take advantage of everyday opportunities to improve spelling skills. By asking your child to read stories or newspaper articles to you at home, or billboards and signs while traveling, you are showing your child how often he or she will encounter these words. You can also give your child extra practice in writing these correct spellings by having him or her write a shopping list or note to a family member.

Since learning to spell can be frustrating, your child may wish to use one or more of the spelling strategies on page 6 when he or she finds a word or group of words difficult to master. You can also encourage your child to use the following study steps to learn a word:

**1.** Say the word. What consonant sounds do you hear? What vowel sounds do you hear? How many syllables do you hear?

**2.** Look at the letters in the word. Think about how each sound is spelled. Find any spelling patterns or parts that you know. Close your eyes. Picture the word in your mind.

**3.** Spell the word aloud.

**4.** Write the word. Say each letter as you write it.

**5.** Check the spelling. If you did not spell the word correctly, use the study steps again.

With help from you and this workbook, your child is well on the way to excellent skills in spelling, reading, and writing!

# table of contents

# spelling strategies

**What can you do when you aren't sure how to spell a word?**

Say the word aloud. Make sure you say it correctly. Listen to the sounds in the word. Think about letters and patterns that might spell the sounds.

Look in the Spelling Table on page 141 to find common spellings for sounds in the word.

Think about related words. They may help you spell the word you're not sure of.

child—children

Guess the spelling of the word and check it in a dictionary.

Write the word in different ways. Compare the spellings and choose the one that looks correct.

trane    tran    (train)    trayn

Think about any spelling rules you know that can help you spell the word.

Most plural words are formed by adding -s.

Choose a rhyming helper and use it. A rhyming helper is a word that rhymes with the word and is spelled like it.

strong—song

Break the word into syllables and think about how each syllable might be spelled.

No-vem-ber
for-got

Create a memory clue, such as a rhyme.

Write i before e, except after c.

# Proofreading Marks

| Mark | Meaning | Example |
|------|---------|---------|
| ⬭ | spell correctly | I ⬭liek⬭ dogs. |
| ⊙ | add period | They are my favorite kind of pet⊙ |
| ? | add question mark | What kind of pet do you have? |
| ≡ | capitalize | My dog's name is <u>scooter</u>.<br>≡ |
| ℓ | take out | He likes to ~~to~~ run and play. |
| ¶ | indent paragraph | ¶I love my dog Scooter. He is the best pet I have ever had. Every morning he wakes me with a bark. Every night he sleeps with me. |
| ⌄⌄ | add quotation marks | ⌄You are my best friend,⌄ I tell him. |

# Words with Short a

| | | | |
|---|---|---|---|
| ask | matter | black | add |
| match | Saturday | class | apple |
| subtract | laugh | thank | catch |
| January | after | hammer | half |

**catch**

## Say and Listen

Say each spelling word. Listen for the short *a* sound.

## Think and Sort

Look at the letters in each word. Think about how short *a* is spelled. Spell each word aloud.

Short *a* can be shown as /ă/. How many spelling patterns for /ă/ do you see?

1. Write the **fifteen** spelling words that have the *a* pattern, like *match*.

2. Write the **one** spelling word that has the *au* pattern.

**1. a Words**

_____    _____

_____    _____

_____    _____

_____    _____

_____    _____

_____    _____

_____    **2. au Word**

_____    _____

_____

## Definitions

Write the spelling word for each definition.
Use a dictionary if you need to.

1. to find the sum          _____
2. problem                  _____
3. to look alike            _____
4. group of students        _____
5. following                _____
6. to say one is grateful   _____
7. one of two equal parts   _____
8. to request               _____

## Classifying

Write the spelling word that belongs in each group.

9.  banana       orange     pear        _____
10. add          multiply   divide      _____
11. screwdriver  saw        drill       _____
12. white        green      yellow      _____
13. chuckle      grin       smile       _____
14. March        April      September   _____
15. run          throw      pitch       _____

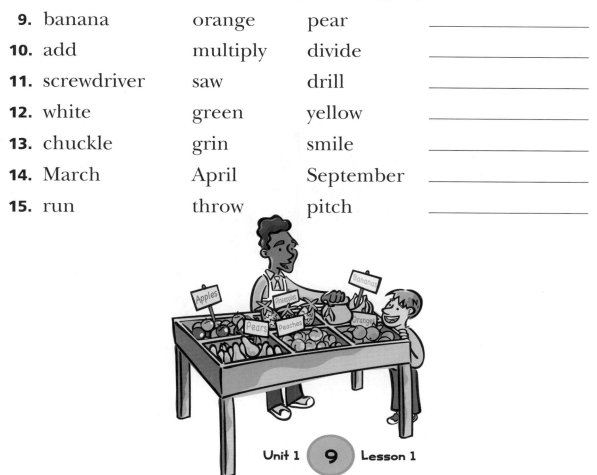

| | | | |
|---|---|---|---|
| ask | matter | black | add |
| match | Saturday | class | apple |
| subtract | laugh | thank | catch |
| January | after | hammer | half |

## Proofreading

Proofread the ad for apple juice below. Use proofreading marks to correct five spelling mistakes, three capitalization mistakes, and two punctuation mistakes. See the chart on page 7 to learn how to use the proofreading marks.

**Proofreading Marks**

⬭ spell correctly
☰ capitalize
⊙ add period

It's Janary You have the sniffles. did you

cach a cold? to feel better fast, drink this.

It is the finest fruit

juice ever made.

Look for the aple

on the bottle. you

will feel great

affter only haf

a glass

Apple Juice

# Dictionary Skills

## Alphabetical Order

When words are in alphabetical order, they are in **ABC** order.

This group of words is in alphabetical order.

> *bend*      *friend*      *horse*

This group of words is <u>not</u> in alphabetical order.

> *egg*      *animal*      *chicken*

Write the following groups of words in alphabetical order.

**1.** matter    January    hammer

_____

_____

_____

**2.** add    match    class

_____

_____

_____

**3.** thank    ask    Saturday

_____

_____

_____

**4.** black    subtract    laugh

_____

_____

_____

# Words with Long a

| | | | |
|---|---|---|---|
| gray | page | great | change |
| April | face | save | away |
| break | ate | place | pay |
| late | safe | May | came |

April

## Say and Listen

Say each spelling word. Listen for the long a sound.

## Think and Sort

Look at the letters in each word. Think about how long a is spelled. Spell each word aloud.

Long a can be shown as /ā/. How many spelling patterns for /ā/ do you see?

1. Write the **nine** spelling words that have the a-consonant-e pattern, like *face.*

2. Write the **four** spelling words that have the ay pattern, like *May.*

3. Write the **two** spelling words that have the ea pattern, like *break.*

4. Write the **one** spelling word that has the a pattern.

**1. a-consonant-e Words**
_____
_____
_____
_____
_____
_____

**2. ay Words**
_____
_____

**3. ea Words**
_____
_____

**4. a Word**
_____

# Synonyms

Synonyms are words that have the same meaning. Write the spelling word that is a synonym for each word below.

1. arrived _____
2. unhurt _____
3. absent _____
4. put _____
5. messenger _____
6. wonderful _____
7. switch _____
8. silvery _____

# Anagrams

An anagram is a word whose letters can be used to make another word. Write the spelling word that contains the letters of the underlined anagram in each sentence.

9. Jenna's birthday is in the month of yaM. _____
10. The team tea pizza after the game. _____
11. Please do not brake my pencil. _____
12. Ten dollars is too much to yap. _____
13. The bus was tale this morning. _____
14. Let's vase the best for last. _____
15. The baby had a big smile on her cafe. _____

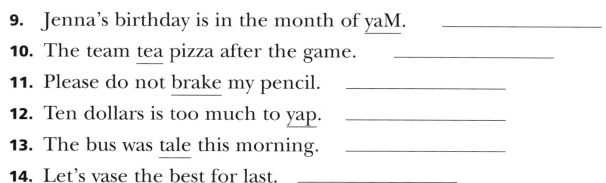

| | | | |
|---|---|---|---|
| gray | page | great | change |
| April | face | save | away |
| break | ate | place | pay |
| late | safe | May | came |

## Proofreading

Proofread these directions for planting a tree. Use proofreading marks to correct five spelling mistakes, three capitalization mistakes, and two unnecessary words.

**Proofreading Marks**

⭕ spell correctly

≡ capitalize

ℓ take out

# How to Plant a Tree

To plant a tree, first choose a saif spot. it should be a playce far from houses and awey from from strong winds. Plant the tree laete in the day when the sun is low. dig a deep hole and save the soil. then put the tree in the hole and water it well. Be careful not to to brek any branches on the tree. Last, pack the soil around the tree.

## Sentences

Begin the first word of each sentence with a capital letter.

*My sister collects postage stamps.*

Put a period at the end of a sentence that tells something.

*The first postage stamp was made in England.*

Use the spelling words in the boxes below to complete the story.
Then use proofreading marks to correct mistakes in the use of capital letters and periods.

| May | face | save | great | page | gray | away |

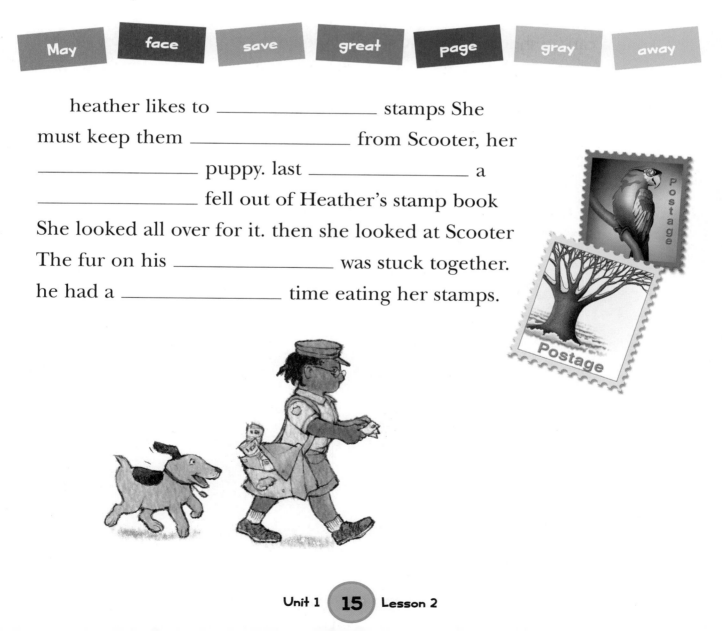

heather likes to _____ stamps She

must keep them _____ from Scooter, her

_____ puppy. last _____ a

_____ fell out of Heather's stamp book

She looked all over for it. then she looked at Scooter

The fur on his _____ was stuck together.

he had a _____ time eating her stamps.

weigh

# More Words with Long a

| | | | |
|---|---|---|---|
| fable | rain | danger | sail |
| afraid | table | aid | train |
| eight | wait | able | aim |
| weigh | they | paint | paper |

## Say and Listen

Say each spelling word. Listen for the long a sound.

## Think and Sort

Look at the letters in each word. Think about how long a is spelled.
Spell each word aloud.

Long a can be shown as /ā/ . How many spelling patterns for /ā/ do you see?

1. Write the **eight** spelling words that have the *ai* pattern, like *rain*.

2. Write the **five** spelling words that have the *a* pattern, like *paper*.

3. Look at the word *eight*. The spelling pattern for this word is *eigh*.
   The *g* and *h* are silent. Write the **two** spelling words that have the
   *eigh* pattern, like *weigh*.

4. Write the **one** spelling word that has the *ey* pattern.

**1. ai** Words

_____

_____

_____

_____    **3. eigh** Words

_____    _____

_____    _____

_____    **4. ey** Word

**2. a** Words    _____

_____

## Antonyms

Antonyms are words that have opposite meanings. Write the spelling word that is an antonym of each word below.

**1.** hurt _____

**2.** fearless _____

**3.** go _____

**4.** safety _____

**5.** unable _____

## Analogies

An analogy shows that one pair of words is like another pair. Write the spelling word that completes each analogy.

**6.** *Bedspread* is to *bed* as *tablecloth* is to _____.

**7.** *Two* is to *four* as *four* is to _____.

**8.** *Car* is to *road* as _____ is to *track*.

**9.** *Engine* is to *car* as _____ is to *sailboat*.

**10.** *Story* is to _____ as *animal* is to *dog*.

**11.** *Silk* is to *smooth* as _____ is to *wet*.

**12.** *We* is to *us* as _____ is to *them*.

**13.** *Oven* is to *bake* as *scale* is to _____.

**14.** *Ink* is to *pen* as _____ is to *brush*.

**15.** *Easy* is to *simple* as _____ is to *point*.

| | | | |
|---|---|---|---|
| fable | rain | danger | sail |
| afraid | table | aid | train |
| eight | wait | able | aim |
| weigh | they | paint | paper |

## Proofreading

Proofread the paragraph below. Use proofreading marks to correct five spelling mistakes, three capitalization mistakes, and two unnecessary words.

**Proofreading Marks**

◯ spell correctly
≡ capitalize
ℓ take out

Mr. sanchez is the art teacher at our school. He teaches the third grade once a week. each class is abel to make many things. This week we are making things out of paper. our class has made a boat with with a large paper sail. Mrs. Digg's class has made a trane that that is aight feet long. Thay cannot wate to paint it.

## Dictionary Skills

### Using the Spelling Table

Suppose that you need to find a word in a dictionary, but you're not sure how to spell one of the sounds. What can you do? You can use a spelling table to find the different ways that the sound can be spelled.

Let's say that you're not sure how to spell the last consonant sound in *sock*. Is it *k, c, ck,* or *ch*? First, find the pronunciation symbol for the sound in the Spelling Table on page 141. Then read the first spelling listed for /k/ and look up *sok* in a dictionary. Look for each spelling in the dictionary until you find the correct one.

| Sound | Spellings | Examples |
|-------|-----------|----------|
| /k/ | k c ck ch | keep, coat, kick, school |

Write the correct spelling for /k/ in each word below. Use the Spelling Table entry above and a dictionary.

**1.** kable _____

**2.** karton _____

**3.** koarse _____

**4.** blak _____

**5.** blok _____

**6.** skeme _____

**7.** komb _____

**8.** subtrakt _____

**9.** klok _____

**10.** kard _____

**11.** korn _____

**12.** soks _____

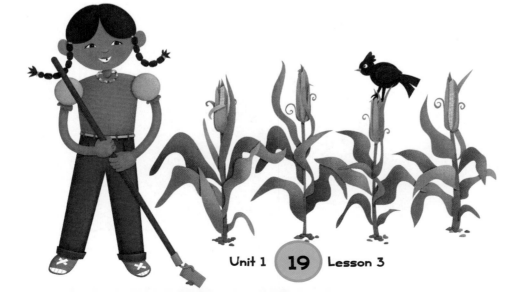

# Words with Short e

| | | | |
|---|---|---|---|
| next | egg | says | ready |
| end | help | spent | again |
| second | forget | dress | said |
| address | read | test | head |

egg

## Say and Listen

Say each spelling word. Listen for the short e sound.

## Think and Sort

Look at the letters in each word. Think about how short e is spelled. Spell each word aloud.

Short e can be shown as /ĕ/. How many spelling patterns for /ĕ/ do you see?

1. Write the **ten** spelling words that have the *e* pattern, like *dress*.

2. Write the **three** spelling words that have the *ea* pattern, like *head*.

3. Write the **two** spelling words that have the *ai* pattern, like *said*.

4. Write the **one** spelling word that has the *ay* pattern.

**1. e Words**

_____

_____

_____

_____

_____

_____

_____

_____

_____

_____

**2. ea Words**

_____

_____

_____

**3. ai Words**

_____

_____

**4. ay Word**

_____

# Clues

Write the spelling word for each clue.

1. includes a ZIP code _____
2. once more _____
3. what is done to a book _____
4. opposite of *remember* _____
5. used your money _____
6. all set _____
7. aid _____
8. I say, you say, he ___ _____

# Classifying

Write the spelling word that belongs in each group.

9. hour        minute        _____
10. exam       quiz          _____
11. spoke      told          _____
12. first      then          _____
13. stop       quit          _____
14. blouse     skirt         _____
15. toast      juice         _____

| | | | |
|---|---|---|---|
| next | egg | says | ready |
| end | help | spent | again |
| second | forget | dress | said |
| address | read | test | head |

## Proofreading

Proofread the journal entry below. Use proofreading marks to correct five spelling mistakes, two capitalization mistakes, and three punctuation mistakes.

**Proofreading Marks**

⬭ spell correctly
≡ capitalize
⊙ add period

October 18

Today I forgot to take my lunch to school. I often forgit things Mom sezs that i need to use my hed. she gave me some string and told me about a trick that will healp I will use the string to tie a bow around my secund finger The bow will help me remember my lunch.

## Multiple Meanings

Many words have more than one meaning. If an entry word in a dictionary has more than one meaning, the different meanings are numbered. Read the dictionary entry below.

> **then** (thĕn) *adverb* **1.** At the time: *I used to sleep with a teddy bear, but I was only a baby then.* **2.** After that: *We saw lightning flash, and then we heard the thunder roar.* **3.** A time mentioned: *Go finish your homework, and by then dinner will be ready.*

**1.** What is the entry word? _____

**2.** How many meanings does the word have? _____

Write the words *egg, address, next,* and *help* in alphabetical order. Then look them up in the dictionary. Write the page on which each entry appears. Then write the number of meanings each word has.

|  | Word | Page | Number of Meanings |
|---|---|---|---|
| **3.** | _____ | _____ | _____ |
| **4.** | _____ | _____ | _____ |
| **5.** | _____ | _____ | _____ |
| **6.** | _____ | _____ | _____ |

# Plural Words

| | | | |
|---|---|---|---|
| tests | pages | papers | dresses |
| hammers | tables | clowns | classes |
| paints | apples | eggs | matches |
| hands | trains | addresses | places |

## Say and Listen

Say the spelling words. Listen for the ending sounds.

## Think and Sort

All of the spelling words are plural words. **Plural** words name more than one thing. Most plural words are formed by adding -s.

boy + **s** = boy**s**      page + **s** = page**s**

**Singular** words name one thing. If a singular word ends in *s, ss, ch,* or *x, -es* is added to form the plural.

glass + **es** = glass**es**

1. Write the **twelve** spelling words that are formed by adding -s, like *tests*.

2. Write the **four** spelling words that are formed by adding -es, like *dresses*.

1. -s Plurals

_____      _____

_____      _____

_____      

_____      2. -es Plurals

_____      _____

_____      _____

_____      _____

_____

## Making Connections

Complete each sentence with the spelling word that goes with the workers.

1. Artists use brushes and _____.

2. Carpenters work with nails and _____.

3. Fruit farmers grow oranges and _____.

4. Cooks work with milk and _____.

5. Teachers grade projects and _____.

6. Writers work with _____ in books.

7. Tailors sew skirts and _____.

8. Mail carriers work with names and _____.

## Definitions

Write the spelling word for each definition.
Use a dictionary if you need to.

9. questions that measure knowledge _____

10. small sticks of wood used to light fires _____

11. connected railroad cars _____

12. part of the arms below the wrists _____

13. particular areas _____

14. circus performers who make people laugh _____

15. groups of students taught by the same teacher _____

| | | | |
|---|---|---|---|
| tests | pages | papers | dresses |
| hammers | tables | clowns | classes |
| paints | apples | eggs | matches |
| hands | trains | addresses | places |

## Proofreading

Proofread the movie review below. Use proofreading marks to correct five spelling mistakes, three capitalization mistakes, and two punctuation mistakes.

**Proofreading Marks**
- ◯ spell correctly
- ≡ capitalize
- ⊙ add period

# MOVIE REVIEW

Do you like funny movies? If you do, you will love *Pagess from Our Lives*. it is the story of a group of clownes as they travel to different playces all over the world They use apples and egges to teach juggling to children at a school in France. they also dance on tabels at a park in China. you will have a great time at this movie Your parents will like it, too.

## Dictionary Skills

## Base Words

A base word is a word from which other words are formed. For example, *apple* is the base word in *apples*, and *test* is the base word in *tests*.

Many entry words in a dictionary are base words. Different forms of a base word may be listed in the entry. The different forms are printed in dark type. Look up the word *dress* in a dictionary. How many different forms of *dress* does the entry show? What are they?

Write the following words in alphabetical order. Write the base word for each word. Then find the base word in the dictionary. Write the number of different forms given for the word.

hands    addresses    trains    pages    paints

| Word | Base Word | Number of Word Forms |
|------|-----------|----------------------|
| 1. _____ | _____ | _____ |
| 2. _____ | _____ | _____ |
| 3. _____ | _____ | _____ |
| 4. _____ | _____ | _____ |
| 5. _____ | _____ | _____ |

# unit 1 Review
## Lessons 1–5

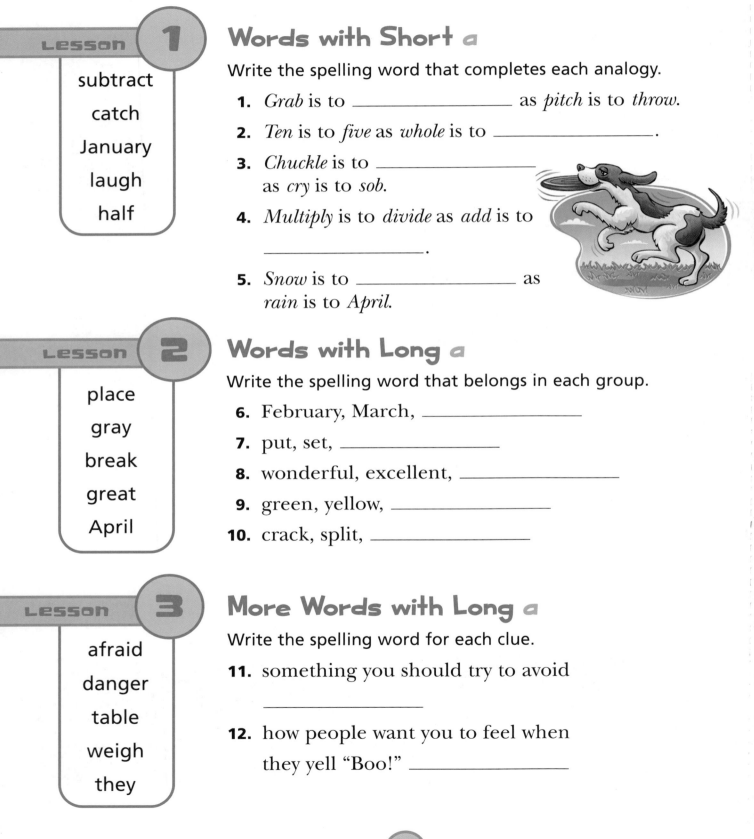

### LESSON 1

subtract
catch
January
laugh
half

## Words with Short a

Write the spelling word that completes each analogy.

1. *Grab* is to _____ as *pitch* is to *throw*.

2. *Ten* is to *five* as *whole* is to _____.

3. *Chuckle* is to _____ as *cry* is to *sob*.

4. *Multiply* is to *divide* as *add* is to _____.

5. *Snow* is to _____ as *rain* is to *April*.

### LESSON 2

place
gray
break
great
April

## Words with Long a

Write the spelling word that belongs in each group.

6. February, March, _____
7. put, set, _____
8. wonderful, excellent, _____
9. green, yellow, _____
10. crack, split, _____

### LESSON 3

afraid
danger
table
weigh
they

## More Words with Long a

Write the spelling word for each clue.

11. something you should try to avoid _____

12. how people want you to feel when they yell "Boo!" _____

**13.** a word that can be used to name others

_____

**14.** what scales are used for   _____

**15.** what you set before a meal and sit at to
eat the meal   _____

LESSON **4**

## Words with Short e

address
second
ready
again
says

Write the spelling word that completes each sentence.

**16.** Are you _____ for school?

**17.** If my hair is still messy, I need to comb
it _____.

**18.** My mother _____, "Clean up
your room, please."

**19.** At the end of the race, Mario was in
_____ place.

**20.** Your street, town, and ZIP code are parts
of your _____

LESSON **5**

## Plural Words

eggs
hammers
places
apples
matches

Write the spelling word that answers each question.

**21.** What are red, round, and juicy? _____

**22.** What do hens lay? _____

**23.** What tools are good for pounding nails?

_____

**24.** Which word rhymes with _spaces_?

_____

**25.** What can be used to light fires?

_____

# More Words with Short e

| | | | |
|---|---|---|---|
| slept | February | them | never |
| when | many | sent | kept |
| September | best | friend | then |
| cents | Wednesday | guess | better |

cents

## Say and Listen

Say each spelling word. Listen for the short e sound.

## Think and Sort

Look at the letters in each word. Think about how short e is spelled. Spell each word aloud.

Short e can be shown as /ĕ/. How many spelling patterns for /ĕ/ do you see?

1. Write the **thirteen** spelling words that have the *e* pattern, like *best*.

2. Write the **one** spelling word that has the *ie* pattern.

3. Write the **one** spelling word that has the *a* pattern.

4. Write the **one** spelling word that has the *ue* pattern.

**1. e Words**

_____        _____

_____        _____

_____        _____

_____        **2. ie Word**

_____        _____

_____        **3. a Word**

_____        _____

_____        **4. ue Word**

_____

# Classifying

Write the spelling word that belongs in each group.

1. lots      several    _____
2. pal      buddy    _____
3. July      August    _____
4. Monday      Tuesday    _____
5. rested      napped    _____
6. December      January    _____
7. good      better    _____
8. mailed      shipped    _____
9. who      what    _____

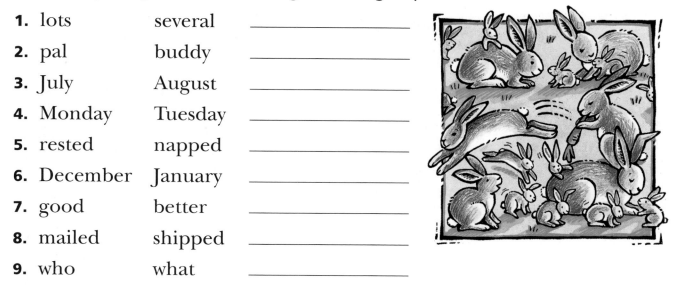

# Rhymes

Write the spelling word that completes each sentence
and rhymes with the underlined word.

10. If you don't have a pen, _____ I will lend you one.

11. No one slept because the dog _____ us up.

12. Tell _____ to hem the curtains.

13. Have you ever read a _____ letter?

14. Let me _____ who made this mess.

15. I _____ knew you were so clever.

| | | | |
|---|---|---|---|
| slept | February | them | never |
| when | many | sent | kept |
| September | best | friend | then |
| cents | Wednesday | guess | better |

## Proofreading

Proofread the e-mail below. Use proofreading marks to correct five spelling mistakes, three capitalization mistakes, and two punctuation mistakes.

**Proofreading Marks**

◯ spell correctly

≡ capitalize

? add question mark

---

**e-mail**

New   Read   File   Delete   Search   Contacts   Check

Ben,

My frend Kim has two goldfish named Spike and

Mike. She keeps thim in a big fishbowl. Last february

Kim went to texas to visit her grandmother. Can you

gess what I did I kep her fish at my house. They were

fun to watch and take care of. kim was happy that her

fish were safe. Can I watch your fish in Saptember

Your friend,

Gwen

## Language Connection

## Capital Letters

Use a capital letter to begin the names of people and pets and to write the word *I*. Also use a capital letter to begin the first word of a sentence.

The following sentences have capitalization errors.
Write each sentence correctly.

**1.** the book i like best was written by fred gibson.

_____

**2.** it is about a dog called old yeller.

_____

**3.** travis and old yeller have many adventures.

_____

**4.** carl anderson wrote about a horse named blaze.

_____

**5.** blaze was kept by a boy named billy.

_____

**6.** a horse named thunderbolt became friends with billy and blaze.

_____

# Words with Long e

| | | | |
|---|---|---|---|
| street | please | free | wheel |
| read | queen | each | sneeze |
| people | meet | team | sea |
| need | dream | sleep | meat |

queen

## Say and Listen

Say each spelling word. Listen for the long e sound.

## Think and Sort

Look at the letters in each word. Think about how long e is spelled. Spell each word aloud.

Long e can be shown as /ē/. How many spelling patterns for /ē/ do you see?

**1.** Write the **eight** spelling words that have the *ee* pattern, like *meet*.

**2.** Write the **seven** spelling words that have the *ea* pattern, like *team*.

**3.** Write the **one** spelling word that has the *eo* pattern.

**1. e Words**

_____
_____
_____
_____
_____
_____
_____
_____

**2. ea Words**

_____
_____
_____
_____
_____
_____

**3. eo Word**

_____

# Analogies

Write the spelling word that completes each analogy.

1. *Sit* is to *chair* as _____ is to *bed*.

2. *Train* is to *track* as *car* is to _____.

3. *Hives* are to *bees* as *houses* are to _____.

4. *Cough* is to *mouth* as _____ is to *nose*.

5. *Book* is to _____ as *movie* is to *watch*.

6. *Rectangle* is to *door* as *circle* is to _____.

7. *Bush* is to *shrub* as *ocean* is to _____.

# Definitions

Write the spelling word for each definition.
Use a dictionary if you need to.

8. food from the flesh of animals _____

9. a group of people playing on the same side _____

10. to think, feel, or see during sleep _____

11. to come together _____

12. without cost _____

13. to give pleasure or happiness to _____

14. every one _____

15. must have _____

| | | | |
|---|---|---|---|
| street | please | free | wheel |
| read | queen | each | sneeze |
| people | meet | team | sea |
| need | dream | sleep | meat |

## Proofreading

Proofread the book jacket below. Use proofreading marks to correct five spelling mistakes, three capitalization mistakes, and two unnecessary words.

**Proofreading Marks**

◯ spell correctly
≡ capitalize
ℓ take out

Readers will love this new story about a

young queen.  one day she has a a strange dream.

In the dream, she is on a baseball teme.  each time

she gets up to bat, a sea of of peeple cheer her.

The queen hits four home runs.  after the game,

she wants to mete ech fan.  Rede this exciting tale

to learn what happens when the queen wakes up.

## Nouns

A noun is a word that names a person, place, thing, or idea. The following words are nouns.

| Person | Place | Thing | Idea |
|---|---|---|---|
| boy | seashore | toy | beauty |
| girl | forest | dog | peace |

Write the sentences below, completing them with the correct nouns from the boxes.

| meat | wheel | sea | dream | people | street |
|---|---|---|---|---|---|

**1.** I had a wonderful ___ last night.

_____

**2.** All the ___ who live on my ___ were in it.

_____

**3.** I used a big ___ to steer our big ship out to ___.

_____

**4.** We had a feast of fruit and roasted ___ on an island.

_____

# More Words with Long e

| | | | |
|---|---|---|---|
| only | story | key | family |
| sleepy | carry | sunny | these |
| funny | very | every | city |
| penny | even | happy | busy |

city

## Say and Listen

Say each spelling word. Listen for the long e sound.

## Think and Sort

Look at the letters in each word. Think about how long e is spelled. Spell each word aloud.

Long e can be shown as /ē/. How many spelling patterns for /ē/ do you see?

1. Write the **one** spelling word that has the *e* pattern.

2. Write the **thirteen** spelling words that have the *y* pattern, like *story*.

3. Write the **one** spelling word that has the *e*-consonant-*e* pattern.

4. Write the **one** spelling word that has the *ey* pattern.

**1. e Word**

_____

**2. y Words**

_____    _____

_____    _____

_____    _____

_____    _____

_____    **3. e-consonant-e Word**

_____    _____

_____    **4. ey Word**

_____

## Definitions

Write the spelling word for each definition.
Use a dictionary if you need to.

1. to take from one place to another _____

2. extremely _____

3. the most important part _____

4. laughable _____

5. each _____

6. one cent _____

7. nearby items _____

8. a telling of something that happened _____

9. just _____

## Antonyms

Write the spelling word that is an antonym of the underlined word.

10. Seth was sad when summer camp began. _____

11. We will go to the zoo on a cloudy day. _____

12. Saturday was a lazy day for everyone. _____

13. Life in the country can be very exciting. _____

14. Kara felt lively after reading a book. _____

15. Twelve is an odd number. _____

| | | | |
|---|---|---|---|
| only | story | key | family |
| sleepy | carry | sunny | these |
| funny | very | every | city |
| penny | even | happy | busy |

## Proofreading

Proofread the letter below. Use proofreading marks to correct five spelling mistakes, three capitalization mistakes, and two punctuation mistakes.

**Proofreading Marks**

◯ spell correctly

≡ capitalize

⊙ add period

306 Maple Drive

Campbell, CA  95011

November 10, 2004

Dear Tina,

   My mom got a new job. she is going to be a firefighter in the big citty of Chicago, Illinois Our familee is very hapy. we have been buzy packing since early thursday morning I will write again verry soon and tell you more.

   Your cousin,

   Tasha

## Dictionary Skills

## Alphabetical Order

The words in a dictionary are in alphabetical order.
Use a dictionary to complete the following sentences.

1. Words that begin with **A** start on page _____ and
   end on page _____.

2. Words that begin with **M** start on page _____ and
   end on page _____.

3. Words that begin with **W** start on page _____ and
   end on page _____.

Write the words below in alphabetical order. Then find each
one in the dictionary and write its page number.

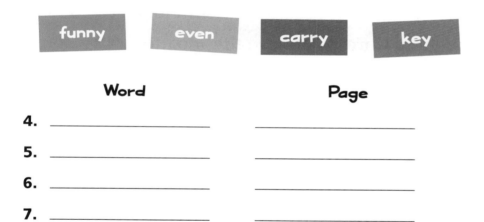

| Word | Page |
|------|------|
| 4. _____ | _____ |
| 5. _____ | _____ |
| 6. _____ | _____ |
| 7. _____ | _____ |

# Words with Short u

| | | | |
|---|---|---|---|
| from | Sunday | money | under |
| nothing | summer | does | mother |
| lunch | month | such | front |
| much | sun | other | Monday |

**sun**

## Say and Listen

Say each spelling word. Listen for the short *u* sound.

## Think and Sort

Look at the letters in each word. Think about how short *u* is spelled. Spell each word aloud.

Short *u* can be shown as /ŭ/. How many spelling patterns for /ŭ/ do you see?

1. Write the **seven** spelling words that have the *u* pattern, like *sun*.

2. Write the **one** spelling word that has the *oe* pattern.

3. Write the **eight** spelling words that have the *o* pattern, like *month*.

**1. u Words**

_____
_____
_____
_____
_____
_____
_____

**2. oe Word**

_____

**3. o Words**

_____
_____
_____
_____
_____
_____
_____
_____

# Letter Scramble

Unscramble the underlined letters to make
a spelling word. Write the word on the line.

1. Kelly was at the <u>tronf</u> of the line.  _____

2. We hid the keys <u>drune</u> the mat.  _____

3. How much <u>noemy</u> is in your pocket?  _____

4. We had never seen <u>chus</u> a mess.  _____

5. We could see <u>honnitg</u> in the dark.  _____

6. When <u>osde</u> the bus come?  _____

# Clues

Write the spelling word for each clue.

7. The first one is January.  _____

8. This day comes before Tuesday.  _____

9. This word is the opposite of *to*.  _____

10. When it shines, you feel warmer.  _____

11. This day comes after Saturday.  _____

12. This person has at least one son or daughter.  _____

13. If you have this, you have a lot.  _____

14. This season contains June, July, and August.  _____

15. This word means "different."  _____

| | | | |
|---|---|---|---|
| *from* | *Sunday* | *money* | *under* |
| *nothing* | *summer* | *does* | *mother* |
| *lunch* | *month* | *such* | *front* |
| *much* | *sun* | *other* | *Monday* |

## Proofreading

Proofread the e-mail message below. Use proofreading marks to correct five spelling mistakes, three capitalization mistakes, and two punctuation mistakes.

**Proofreading Marks**

◯ spell correctly

≡ capitalize

? add question mark

**e-mail**

| New | Read | File | Delete | Search | Contacts ... ck |
|---|---|---|---|---|---|

Dear Grandpa,

Thank you for the soccer ball and mony you gave

me for my birthday on Munday. Somer begins in only

one more month. Can you believe it  I am going to play

soccer in our frunt yard every day. each sunday I will

come to your house. We can sit in the sun and eat

lonch. We'll have fun! does that sound good to you

Josh

## Question Marks

Use a question mark at the end of a sentence that asks a question.

Do you like riddles?    Can you answer these?

your teeth

your lap

the letter <u>m</u>

Write each riddle correctly. Then choose one of the answers in the boxes to the right and write it in the space provided.

**1.** What comes once in a month, twice in a moment, but never in a hundred years

_____

_____

Answer: _____

**2.** What do you lose whenever you stand up

_____

Answer: _____

**3.** What can you put into the apple pie you have for lunch

_____

Answer: _____

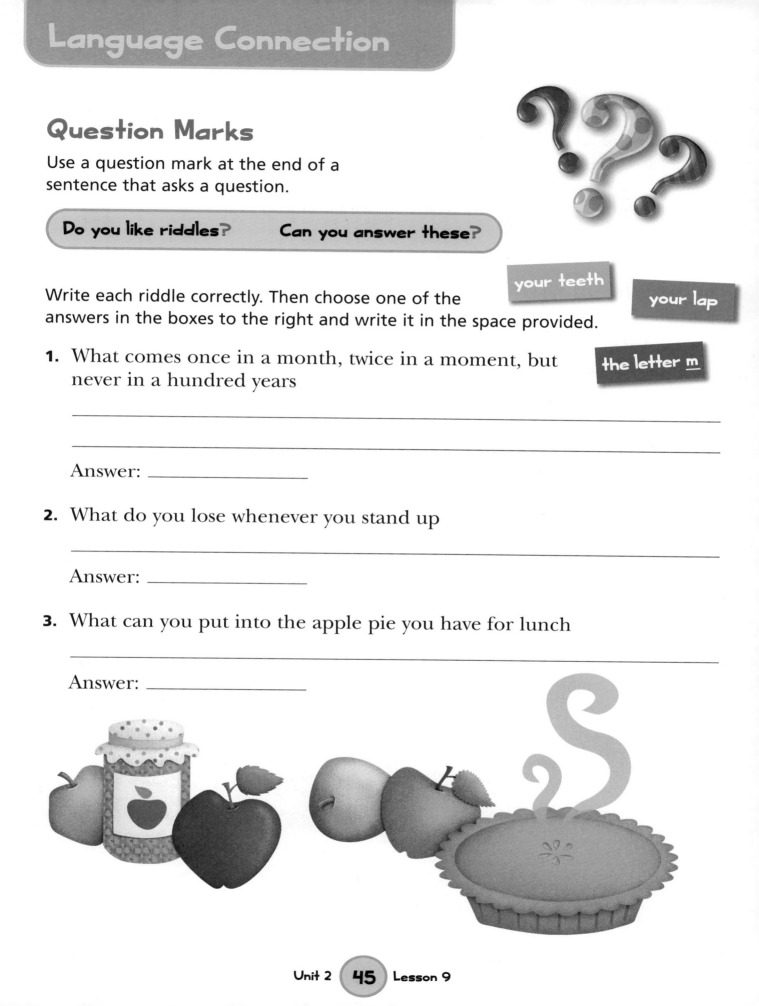

# Contractions

| | | | |
|---|---|---|---|
| she's | they'll | I've | you'll |
| we've | I'm | I'll | you've |
| it's | I'd | you'd | we'll |
| they'd | she'll | they've | he's |

we've

## Say and Listen

Say the spelling words. Listen to the ending sounds.

## Think and Sort

Each spelling word is a **contraction**. Two words are joined, but one or more letters are left out. An apostrophe (') is used in place of the missing letters.

*Had* and *would* are written the same way in contractions. So are *is* and *has*.

1. Write the **five** spelling words that are *will* contractions, like *we'll*.

2. Write the **four** spelling words that are *have* contractions, like *you've*.

3. Write the **three** spelling words that are *would* or *had* contractions, like *they'd*.

4. Write the **three** spelling words that are *is* or *has* contractions, like *she's*.

5. Write the **one** spelling word that is an *am* contraction.

**1. will** Contractions

_____

_____

_____

_____

**2. have** Contractions

_____

_____

_____

**3. would** or **had** Contractions

_____

_____

**4. is** or **has** Contractions

_____

_____

_____

**5. am** Contractions

_____

# Trading Places

Write the contraction that could be used instead of the underlined words in each sentence.

1. It is time to eat. _____
2. I have seen the world's tallest building. _____
3. He is feeling tired. _____
4. You will like my uncle's farm. _____
5. You have grown so tall! _____
6. They would be happy to see you. _____
7. They have found their ball. _____
8. We will make dinner together. _____
9. We have finished painting. _____

# Rhymes

Write the spelling word that completes each sentence and rhymes with the underlined word.

10. A dime is what _____ looking for.
11. Did you hear Kara sneeze? _____ got a cold.
12. If the children see a whale, _____ be excited.
13. The seal is hungry, so _____ feed it.
14. Let's buy food that _____ like to eat.
15. While you nap, _____ read a book.

**Contractions**

| she's | they'll | I've | you'll |
|-------|---------|------|--------|
| we've | I'm | I'll | you've |
| it's | I'd | you'd | we'll |
| they'd | she'll | they've | he's |

## Proofreading

Proofread the journal entry below.
Use proofreading marks to correct five
spelling mistakes, two capitalization
mistakes, and three punctuation mistakes.

**Proofreading Marks**

◯ spell correctly
≡ capitalize
⊙ add period

November 14

My friend pete and I found a lost dog today. I'me not

sure whose puppy it is. Pete thought that I'dd know

because I know all the dogs in the neighborhood He's

really worried about the pup. It's white with black spots.

Wev' put up signs about finding a lost puppy. I'v even

called Chief collins at the police station

We'l be glad when we find the owner

## Contractions

At least one letter and sound are missing from every contraction. An apostrophe (') shows where the letter or letters have been left out. For example, in the contraction *we've*, the apostrophe shows that the letters *ha* have been left out.

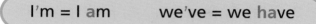

I'm = I am          we've = we have

Write the contraction for each pair of words. Then write the letter or letters that are left out.

| | Contraction | Letter or Letters Left Out |
|---|---|---|
| **1.** I will | _____ | _____ |
| **2.** he is | _____ | _____ |
| **3.** it is | _____ | _____ |
| **4.** they have | _____ | _____ |
| **5.** you had | _____ | _____ |
| **6.** I am | _____ | _____ |
| **7.** you would | _____ | _____ |
| **8.** she has | _____ | _____ |

# unit 2 Review
## Lessons 6-10

Wednesday
February
friend
many
guess

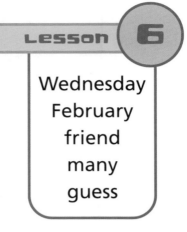

## More Words with Short e

Write the spelling word that completes each analogy.

1. *Pal* is to _____ as *chilly* is to *cold.*

2. *Saturday* is to *end* as _____ is to *middle.*

3. *Know* is to *understand* as *suppose* is to

   _____.

4. *Little* is to *few* as *much* is to

   _____.

5. *Monday* is to *day* as

   _____ is to *month.*

queen
meet
please
team
people

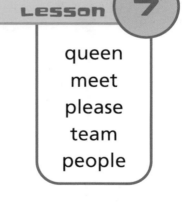

## Words with Long e

Write the spelling word that belongs in each group.

6. duchess   princess   _____

7. group     club       _____

8. persons   humans     _____

9. touch     join       _____

10. delight  cheer      _____

even
every
family
these
key

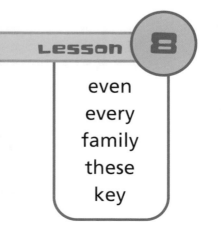

## More Words with Long e

Write the spelling word for each clue.

11. This has parents and children.  _____

12. If a floor is flat, it is this.  _____

13. You can use this word instead of *each.*

    _____

**14.** This can unlock a door or start a car.

_____

**15.** We use this word to point out a group of nearby things. _____

**LESSON** **9**

lunch
such
other
month
does

## Words with Short u

Write the spelling word that completes each sentence.

**16.** My cat always _____ whatever he wants.

**17.** Mom and Dad pay our bills at the end of the _____.

**18.** Do you want this blouse or the _____ one?

**19.** Isaac had soup and a salad for _____ today.

**20.** Dad and I had never seen _____ a big storm.

**LESSON** **10**

she'll
you've
they'd
it's
I'm

## Contractions

Write the spelling word for each word pair.

**21.** I am _____

**22.** you have _____

**23.** she will _____

**24.** they would _____

**25.** it is _____

# More Words with Short u

| lovely | just | something | hundred |
|--------|------|-----------|---------|
| done | some | sum | must |
| shove | won | butter | cover |
| supper | none | number | one |

**supper**

## Say and Listen

Say each spelling word. Listen for the short *u* sound.

## Think and Sort

Look at the letters in each word. Think about how short *u* is spelled. Spell each word aloud.

Short *u* can be shown as /ŭ/. How many spelling patterns for /ŭ/ do you see?

1.  Write the **seven** spelling words that have the *u* pattern, like *must*.

2.  Write the **two** spelling words that have the *o* pattern, like *won*.

3.  Write the **seven** spelling words that have the *o*-consonant-*e* pattern, like *some*.

**1. u Words**

_____

_____

_____

_____

_____

_____

**3. o-consonant-e Words**

_____

_____

_____

_____

_____

_____

**2. o Words**

_____

_____

## Definitions

Write the spelling word for each definition.
Use a dictionary if you need to.

1. gained a victory    _____
2. to put or lay over    _____
3. a particular thing that is not named    _____
4. a certain number of    _____
5. the answer for an addition problem    _____
6. a number, written 1    _____
7. ten groups of ten    _____
8. will have to    _____
9. amount    _____
10. not any    _____

## Synonyms

Complete each sentence by writing the spelling word that is a synonym for the underlined word.

11. Tan's work will soon be finished.    _____
12. Tasha is wearing a beautiful scarf.    _____
13. I'll push Mother's surprise in the closet.    _____
14. No one could argue with the fair law.    _____
15. Kevin ate fish and rice for dinner.    _____

| | | | |
|---|---|---|---|
| lovely | just | something | hundred |
| done | some | sum | must |
| shove | won | butter | cover |
| supper | none | number | one |

## Proofreading

Proofread the journal entry below.
Use proofreading marks to correct five
spelling mistakes, three capitalization
mistakes, and two punctuation mistakes.

**Proofreading Marks**

◯ spell correctly
≡ capitalize
⊙ add period

December 15

yesterday was the best day of my life. I jest
cannot believe that I won something. rocket and I
were nomber one in the show. now we have a lovley
ribbon. There were more than two hunderd people
watching.

I must enter another horse show soon I've never
dun anything as fun as riding in that show. I think
Rocket had fun, too. Dad says that he will take us
to any show in the state

## Homophones

Homophones are words that sound alike but have different spellings and meanings. Look at the homophone pairs in the boxes below. Think about what each homophone means.

one    won        some    sum

ate    eight        son    sun        sail    sale

Use the homophones above to complete each sentence.
Use a dictionary if you need to.

1. The ship must _____ at sunrise.

2. I bought this lovely jacket on _____.

3. Jason _____ some soup and a sandwich for supper.

4. My favorite number is _____.

5. The hot _____ made some of us thirsty.

6. We just met Mrs. Lee's daughter and her _____.

7. Jesse _____ two blue ribbons at the art contest.

8. Mr. Ono owns _____ car and two bicycles.

9. Mari found the _____ of _____ numbers.

# Words with Short i

| | | | |
|---|---|---|---|
| thing | little | winter | kick |
| begin | river | been | dish |
| fill | think | spring | pretty |
| which | December | build | children |

**kick**

## Say and Listen

Say each spelling word. Listen for the short *i* sound.

## Think and Sort

Look at the letters in each word. Think about how short *i* is spelled. Spell each word aloud.

Short *i* can be shown as /ĭ/. How many spelling patterns for /ĭ/ do you see?

**1.** Write the **eleven** spelling words that have the *i* pattern, like *dish*.

**2.** Write the **two** spelling words that have the *e* pattern, like *pretty*.

**3.** Write the **one** spelling word that has the *e* and the *i* patterns.

**4.** Write the **one** spelling word that has the *ui* pattern.

**5.** Write the **one** spelling word that has the *ee* pattern.

**1.** i Words

_____

_____

_____

_____

_____

_____

_____

**2.** e Words

_____

_____

**3.** e and i Word

_____

**4.** ui Word

_____

**5.** ee Word

_____

## Clues

Write the spelling word for each clue.

1. what you do to a soccer ball     _____
2. young people     _____
3. what you do with a hammer and nails _____
4. a big stream     _____
5. a season that can be cold     _____
6. a word that rhymes with *fish*     _____
7. the opposite of *end*     _____
8. a word for *beautiful*     _____
9. the opposite of *big*     _____

## Rhymes

Write the spelling word that completes each sentence and rhymes with the underlined word.

10. I _____ I will wear my <u>pink</u> shirt.

11. The coach told the player _____ <u>pitch</u> was good.

12. If you have not _____ practicing, you will not <u>win</u> the music contest.

13. I will <u>bring</u> you flowers in the _____.

14. Jill will climb the <u>hill</u> and _____ the bucket.

15. <u>Bring</u> that little blue _____ to me.

| thing | little | winter | kick |
|-------|--------|--------|------|
| begin | river | been | dish |
| fill | think | spring | pretty |
| which | December | build | children |

## Proofreading

Proofread the postcard below. Use proofreading marks to correct five spelling mistakes, three capitalization mistakes, and two punctuation mistakes.

**Proofreading Marks**

⬭ spell correctly
≡ capitalize
⊙ add period

Hi, luke!

We had a great time at the pioneer

fair. i saw people buld a barn I learned

that it was hard to be a pioneer in the

winnter. The rivere freezes by Decembr,

and then it is hard to fish. Life is easier

when springe comes. maybe you can

come to the fair with us next year

Dylan

**Luke Babb
158 Beach Drive
Austin, TX 78739**

## Adjectives

An adjective describes a noun or pronoun by telling
which one, what kind, or how many.

> **The spotted pony ate the green grass.**

> **The fresh flowers are lovely.**

Use the adjectives in the boxes below to complete the sentences.
Then circle all the adjectives in the sentences.

| | | | | |
|---|---|---|---|---|
| icy | little | hot | every | dangerous |
| pretty | shallow | many | brown | late |

**1.** A river flows by the simple _____ cabin.

**2.** It travels for _____ miles through the thick forest.

**3.** In the winter the river is cold and _____.

**4.** Thin ice in some places is _____ for skaters.

**5.** Many _____ flowers line the banks in spring.

**6.** On _____ summer days, people wade in the river.

**7.** They walk on large rocks in the _____ water.

**8.** In the fall, red and _____ leaves float down the river.

**9.** The river changes with _____ season.

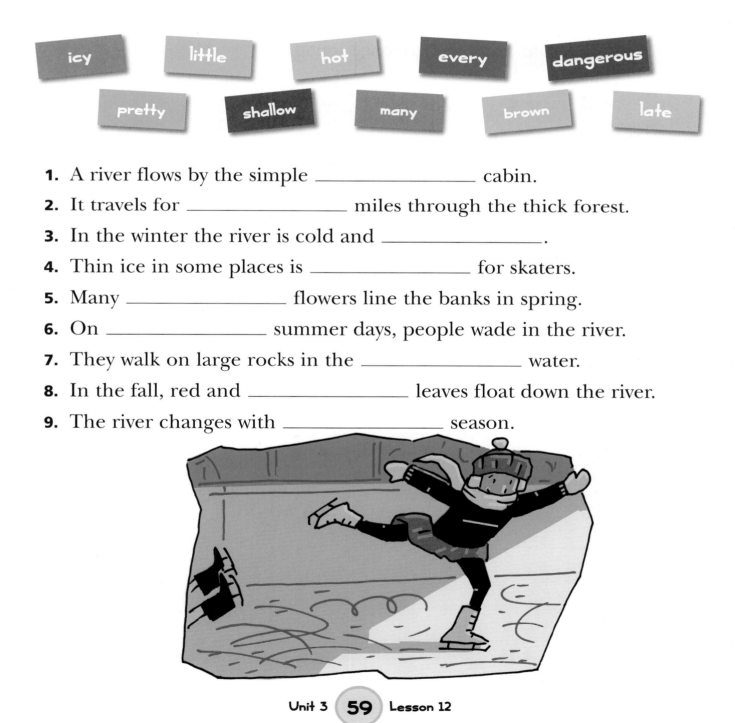

# Words with Long i

| | | | |
|---|---|---|---|
| alike | while | eyes | white |
| line | lion | size | miles |
| times | nice | drive | tiny |
| write | inside | mine | shine |

lion

## Say and Listen

Say each spelling word. Listen for the long *i* sound.

## Think and Sort

Look at the letters in each word. Think about how long *i* is spelled.
Spell each word aloud.

Long *i* can be shown as /ī/. How many spelling patterns for /ī/ do you see?

1. Write the **thirteen** spelling words that have the *i*-consonant-*e*
   pattern, like *nice*.

2. Write the **two** spelling words that have the *i* pattern, like *tiny*.

3. Write the **one** spelling word that has the *eye* pattern.

> **1. i-consonant-e Words**
> _____     _____
> _____     _____
> _____     _____
> _____
> _____     **2. i Words**
> _____     _____
> _____     _____
> _____     **3. eye Word**
> _____     _____

## Clues

Write the spelling word for each clue.

1. what people do with a car                     _____

2. belongs in a group with *feet* and *yards*     _____

3. it can be straight or crooked                  _____

4. a word meaning "at the same time"              _____

5. a word that rhymes with *eyes*                 _____

6. what people do to some shoes                   _____

## Analogies

Write the spelling word that completes each analogy.

7. *Mean* is to _____ as *weak* is to *strong*.

8. *You* is to *me* as *yours* is to _____.

9. *Add* is to *plus* as *multiply* is to _____.

10. *Light* is to *dark* as _____ is to *black*.

11. *Hear* is to *ears* as *see* is to _____.

12. *Needle* is to *sew* as *pen* is to _____.

13. *Small* is to _____ as *big* is to *huge*.

14. *Different* is to *unlike* as *same* is to _____.

15. *Up* is to *down* as _____ is to *outside*.

| | | | |
|---|---|---|---|
| alike | while | eyes | white |
| line | lion | size | miles |
| times | nice | drive | tiny |
| write | inside | mine | shine |

## Proofreading

Proofread the newspaper article below. Use proofreading marks to correct five spelling mistakes, three capitalization mistakes, and two punctuation mistakes.

**Proofreading Marks**

⬭ spell correctly
≡ capitalize
⊙ add period

# Lion Land Big Treat

Lion Land opened over the weekend to wild cheers People came from mils away. they stood in linne for hours to become part of this wildlife adventure. once they got insid, they could not believe their eyez. Lions strolled freely and came right up to the cars. We got just a tiney bit nervous when a lion the size of a horse looked at us through our car window. check out Lion Land for yourself. You won't be disappointed

# Dictionary Skills

## Guide Words

Each page in a dictionary has two words at the top. These words are called guide words. The first guide word is the first entry word on the page. The other guide word is the last entry word on the page. Guide words help you find entry words.

Look at the dictionary page below and find the guide words.

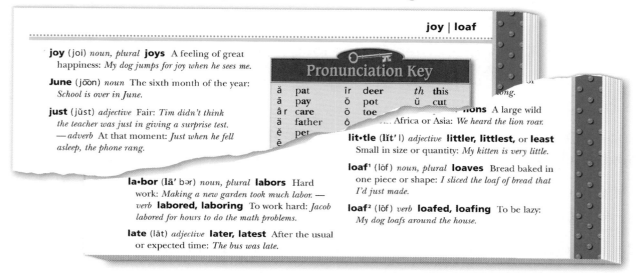

Look up these spelling words in a dictionary. Write the guide words and page number for each.

|  | Guide Words | | Page |
|---|---|---|---|
| **1.** while | _____ | _____ | _____ |
| **2.** drive | _____ | _____ | _____ |
| **3.** nice | _____ | _____ | _____ |
| **4.** size | _____ | _____ | _____ |

# More Words with Long i

| | | | |
|---|---|---|---|
| buy | Friday | fly | kind |
| why | child | mind | try |
| behind | sky | cry | high |
| right | by | light | night |

**cry**

## Say and Listen

Say each spelling word. Listen for the long *i* sound.

## Think and Sort

Look at the letters in each word. Think about how long *i* is spelled. Spell each word aloud.

Long *i* can be shown as /ī/. How many spelling patterns for /ī/ do you see?

1. Write the **five** spelling words that have the *i* pattern, like *kind*.

2. Write the **six** spelling words that have the *y* pattern, like *try*.

3. Write the **four** spelling words that have the *igh* pattern, like *high*.

4. Write the **one** spelling word that has the *uy* pattern.

**1. i** Words

_____

_____

_____

_____

_____

**2. y** Words

_____

_____

_____

**3. igh** Words

_____

_____

_____

_____

**4. uy** Word

_____

# Definitions

Write the spelling word for each definition.
Use a dictionary if you need to.

1. at the back of _____
2. to move through the air _____
3. day before Saturday _____
4. helpful _____
5. next to _____

# Rhymes

Write the spelling word that completes each sentence
and rhymes with the underlined word.

6. My _____ shoe feels too <u>tight</u>.
7. The big box of toys was <u>quite</u> _____.
8. The <u>spy</u> climbed _____ in the tree.
9. The young _____ chose a book about <u>wild</u> animals.
10. Wet or <u>dry</u>, these onions make me _____.
11. Turn on the <u>light</u> to see at _____.
12. Here's a fork so you can _____ my apple <u>pie</u>.
13. What should I _____ my mom for her birthday?
14. Do you _____ if I close the <u>blind</u>?
15. Tell me _____ you used purple <u>dye</u>.

| buy | Friday | fly | kind |
|-----|--------|-----|------|
| why | child | mind | try |
| behind | sky | cry | high |
| right | by | light | night |

## Proofreading

Proofread the e-mail message below. Use proofreading marks to correct five spelling mistakes, three capitalization mistakes, and two punctuation mistakes.

**Proofreading Marks**

◯ spell correctly
≡ capitalize
⊙ add period

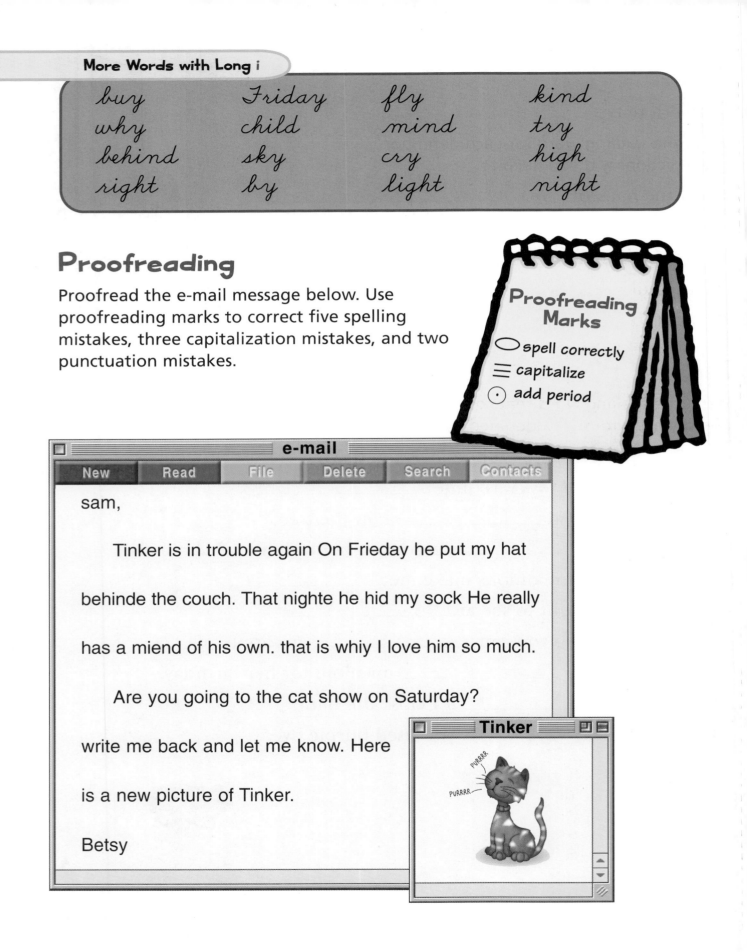

**e-mail**

New | Read | File | Delete | Search | Contacts

sam,

Tinker is in trouble again On Frieday he put my hat

behinde the couch. That nighte he hid my sock He really

has a miend of his own. that is whiy I love him so much.

Are you going to the cat show on Saturday?

write me back and let me know. Here

is a new picture of Tinker.

Betsy

**Tinker**

PURRRR

PURRRA

## Dictionary Skills

## Alphabetical Order

Many words begin with the same letter. To arrange these words in alphabetical order, look at the second letter of each word. Look at the two words below. Then complete the sentences that follow.

sky    story

1. *Sky* and *story* both start with the letter *s*. To put them in alphabetical order, look at the _____ letter.

2. The second letter in *sky* is _____.

3. The second letter in *story* is _____.

4. In the alphabet, *k* comes before *t*, so the word _____ comes before the word _____.

In each list below, the words begin with the same letter. Look at the second letter of each word. Then write the words in alphabetical order.

5. buy    behind    by

_____

_____

_____

6. fly    Friday    finish

_____

_____

_____

# Words with -ed or -ing

| | | | |
|---|---|---|---|
| ending | wished | asked | guessing |
| laughing | dreamed | rained | meeting |
| sleeping | handed | painted | filled |
| reading | subtracted | thanked | waited |

**rained**

## Say and Listen

Say the spelling words.
Listen for the -ed and -ing endings.

## Think and Sort

Each spelling word is formed by adding -ed or -ing to a base word.
A **base word** is a word from which other words are formed. The base word
for *wished* is *wish*. The base word for *ending* is *end*.

Look at each spelling word. Think about the base word and the ending.
Spell each word aloud.

**1.** Write the **ten** spelling words that end in -ed, like *painted*.

**2.** Write the **six** spelling words that end in -ing, like *reading*.

**1. -ed** Words
_____
_____
_____
_____     **2. -ing** Words
_____     _____
_____     _____
_____     _____
_____     _____
                         _____
                         _____

# Definitions

Write the spelling word for each definition.
Use a dictionary if you need to.

1. passed with one's hands    _____
2. said that one was pleased    _____
3. stayed    _____
4. a coming together for some purpose    _____
5. forming an opinion without all the facts    _____
6. saw or thought during sleep    _____
7. fell in drops of water from the clouds    _____

# Analogies

Write the spelling word that completes each analogy.

8. *Taught* is to *instructed* as *hoped* is to _____.
9. *Dress* is to *sewed* as *picture* is to _____.
10. *Playing* is to *piano* as _____ is to *book*.
11. *Chair* is to *sitting* as *bed* is to _____.
12. *Told* is to *explained* as *questioned* is to _____.
13. *Happy* is to _____ as *sad* is to *crying*.
14. *Beginning* is to *start* as _____ is to *finish*.
15. *Out* is to *emptied* as *in* is to _____.

| | | | |
|---|---|---|---|
| *ending* | *wished* | *asked* | *guessing* |
| *laughing* | *dreamed* | *rained* | *meeting* |
| *sleeping* | *handed* | *painted* | *filled* |
| *reading* | *subtracted* | *thanked* | *waited* |

## Proofreading

Proofread the movie review below. Use proofreading marks to correct five spelling mistakes, three capitalization mistakes, and two unnecessary words.

**Proofreading Marks**

⬭ spell correctly
☰ capitalize
ℓ take out

# A Winning Team Is a Winner!

this movie is about a losing hockey team. The coach

has tried everything to to help the team win. he called a

meating each day before practice. He thankt the players

for their hard work but told them he wisht they would

do better. He askt the players to run five miles a day,

even when it it rained.  the surprise endin shows what

really worked.

# End Punctuation

- Use a **period** at the end of a sentence that tells or explains something.
- Use a **question mark** at the end of a sentence that asks a question.
- Use an **exclamation point** at the end of a sentence that shows strong feeling or surprise.

In sentences that have quotation marks, place the end punctuation inside the quotation marks.

> Matt said, "Here comes the team."

> The police officer yelled, "Open that door!"

Write the following sentences, using periods, question marks, and exclamation points correctly.

**1.** Betsy asked Paul, "Who painted this picture"

_____

**2.** She saw that Paul was sleeping

_____

**3.** Betsy shouted, "Boo"

_____

**4.** Paul jumped up fast

_____

**5.** "Oh, Betsy," he cried. "Now I'll never know the ending of my dream"

_____

**6.** They both started laughing

_____

# unit 3 Review
## Lessons 11-15

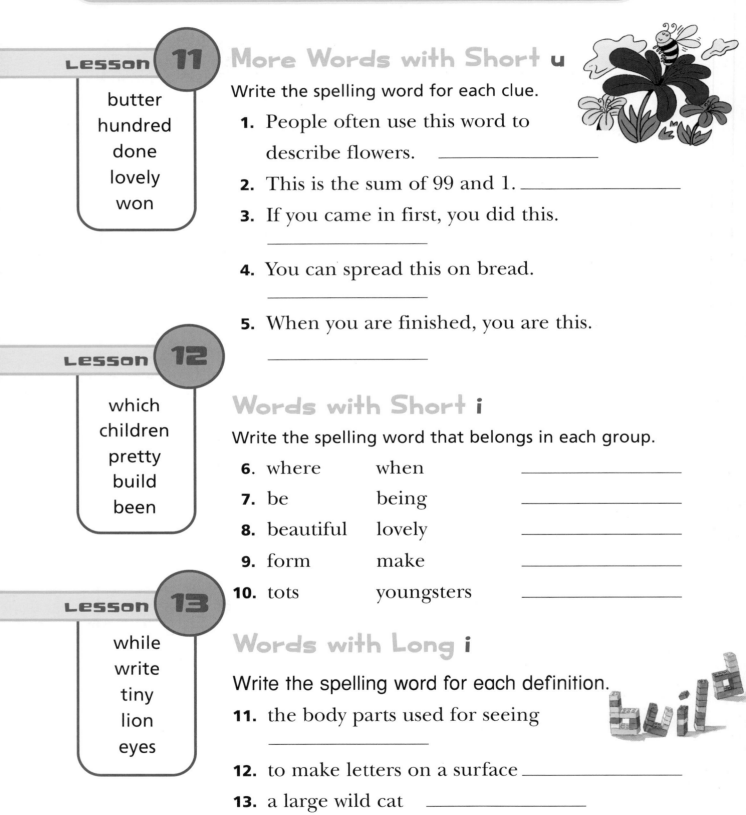

**Lesson 11**

butter
hundred
done
lovely
won

## More Words with Short u

Write the spelling word for each clue.

1. People often use this word to describe flowers. _____

2. This is the sum of 99 and 1. _____

3. If you came in first, you did this. _____

4. You can spread this on bread. _____

5. When you are finished, you are this. _____

**Lesson 12**

which
children
pretty
build
been

## Words with Short i

Write the spelling word that belongs in each group.

6. where        when        _____
7. be           being       _____
8. beautiful    lovely      _____
9. form         make        _____
10. tots        youngsters  _____

**Lesson 13**

while
write
tiny
lion
eyes

## Words with Long i

Write the spelling word for each definition.

11. the body parts used for seeing _____

12. to make letters on a surface _____

13. a large wild cat _____

**14.** although _____

**15.** very small _____

LESSON **14**

behind
why
right
night
buy

## More Words with Long i

Write the spelling word that has the same meaning as the word or words in dark type.

**16. For what reason** did the pioneers go west?

_____

**17.** Can I **pay for** this toy?

_____

**18.** You were **correct** about the weather.

_____

**19.** Last **evening** I had a strange dream.

_____

**20.** Please stand **in back of** me in line.

_____

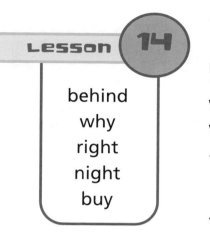

LESSON **15**

wished
thanked
dreamed
guessing
laughing

## Words with -ed or -ing

Write the spelling word that completes each sentence.

**21.** They are _____ at your joke.

**22.** Alicia _____ for a new bicycle.

**23.** Are you just _____ the answer?

**24.** Amad _____ about winning a trophy.

**25.** The teacher _____ the children for the gift.

# Words with Short o

| | | | |
|---|---|---|---|
| October | shop | block | bottle |
| o'clock | sorry | socks | problem |
| what | jog | wash | was |
| clock | bottom | forgot | body |

**shop**

## Say and Listen

Say each spelling word. Listen for the short o sound.

## Think and Sort

Look at the letters in each word. Think about how short o is spelled. Spell each word aloud.

Short o can be shown as /ŏ/. How many spelling patterns for /ŏ/ do you see?

1. Write the **thirteen** spelling words that have the o pattern, like *shop*.

2. Write the **three** spelling words that have the a pattern, like *was*.

**1. o Words**

_____     _____
_____     _____
_____     _____
_____
_____     **2. a Words**
_____     _____
_____     _____

## Clues

Write the spelling word for each clue.

1. clothes that belong on your feet _____

2. has streets on all sides _____

3. in a group with *walk* and *run* _____

4. feeling regret _____

5. a question word _____

6. opposite of *remembered* _____

7. means "of the clock" _____

## Analogies

Write the spelling word that completes each analogy.

8. *Have* is to *has* as *were* is to _____.

9. *Month* is to _____ as *day* is to *Monday*.

10. *Bark* is to *tree* as *skin* is to _____.

11. *Top* is to _____ as *up* is to *down*.

12. *Learn* is to *school* as _____ is to *store*.

13. *Solution* is to _____ as *answer* is to *question*.

14. *Soap* is to _____ as *towel* is to *dry*.

15. *Catsup* is to _____ as *pickle* is to *jar*.

| | | | |
|---|---|---|---|
| October | shop | block | bottle |
| o'clock | sorry | socks | problem |
| what | jog | wash | was |
| clock | bottom | forgot | body |

## Proofreading

Proofread the journal entry below. Use proofreading marks to correct five spelling mistakes, three capitalization mistakes, and two punctuation mistakes.

**Proofreading Marks**

◯ spell correctly
≡ capitalize
⊙ add period

October 18

today I have a mystery to solve. My running sox and hat were at the botom of the stairs when I got home from school Now it is time for my jogg around the blak, but there is a problum. they are both missing. Mom says she didn't move them Nobody is here but Mom and me. Maybe sparky has moved them. I haven't seen that dog since four o'clock.

## Dictionary Skills

## Alphabetical Order

The words *block*, *bottle*, and *butter* begin with the same letter, *b*. To arrange words that begin with the same letter in alphabetical order, use the second letter.

> block     bottle     butter

Write each group of words in alphabetical order.

1. cover     clock     cap     children

   _____

   _____

   _____

   _____

2. shop     salt     sorry     stack

   _____

   _____

   _____

   _____

3. wash     wonder     west     what

   _____

   _____

   _____

   _____

4. forgot     feed     funny     farmer

   _____

   _____

   _____

   _____

# Words with Long o

| | | | |
|---|---|---|---|
| slow | whole | hope | blow |
| joke | wrote | show | yellow |
| goes | toe | alone | hole |
| snow | close | November | know |

**blow**

## Say and Listen

Say each spelling word. Listen for the long o sound.

## Think and Sort

Look at the letters in each word. Think about how long o is spelled. Spell each word aloud.

Long o can be shown as /ō/. How many spelling patterns for /ō/ do you see?

1.  Write the **seven** spelling words that have the *o-consonant-e* pattern, like *hope*.

2.  Write the **six** spelling words that have the *ow* pattern, like *slow*.

3.  Write the **two** spelling words that have the *oe* pattern, like *toe*.

4.  Write the **one** spelling word that has the *o* pattern.

**1. o-consonant-e Words**

_____    _____

_____    _____

_____    _____

_____    _____

_____    **3. oe Words**

_____    _____

**2. ow Words**              _____

_____    **4. o Word**

_____

# Definitions

Write the spelling word for each definition.
Use a dictionary if you need to.

**1.** moves; travels          _____

**2.** made words with a pen   _____

**3.** to wish for something   _____

**4.** the entire amount       _____

**5.** to be familiar with     _____

**6.** by oneself              _____

# Analogies

Write the spelling word that completes each analogy.

**7.** *Shape* is to *square* as *color* is to _____.

**8.** *Lose* is to *win* as _____ is to *open*.

**9.** *January* is to *February* as _____ is to *December*.

**10.** *Hand* is to *finger* as *foot* is to _____.

**11.** *Hot* is to *fire* as *cold* is to _____.

**12.** *Beat* is to *drum* as _____ is to *whistle*.

**13.** *Write* is to *letter* as *dig* is to _____.

**14.** *Rabbit* is to *fast* as *tortoise* is to _____.

**15.** *Day* is to *night* as _____ is to *hide*.

| | | | |
|---|---|---|---|
| slow | whole | hope | blow |
| joke | wrote | show | yellow |
| goes | toe | alone | hole |
| snow | close | November | know |

## Proofreading

Proofread the letter below. Use proofreading marks to correct five spelling mistakes, three capitalization mistakes, and two punctuation mistakes.

**Proofreading Marks**

◯ spell correctly

≡ capitalize

⊙ add period

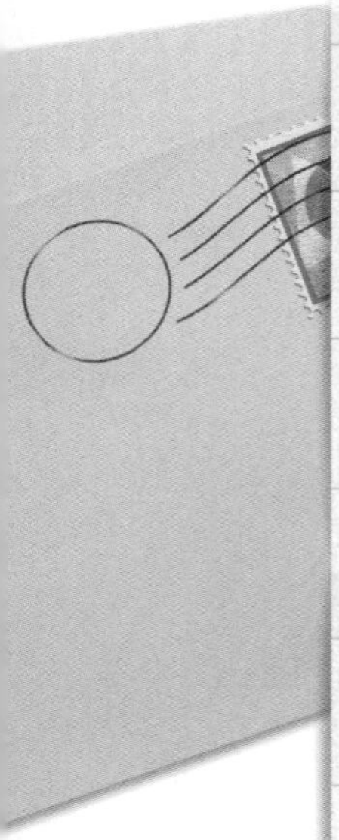

214 Spring Street

Flint Hill, VA 22627

November 29, 2004

Dear Joe,

I kno I haven't written lately. i hoppe you

are not mad. thanks for the yello sweater It

gose great with my blue jacket.

Here's a good joke. why did the pill wear a

blanket? It was a cold tablet

Moe

## Verbs

Action words are called verbs. The spelling words in the boxes are verbs.

Unscramble the letters of the spelling words in the sentences below. Write each sentence and then circle the verb.

| wrote |
| goes |
| know |

**1.** Jack hurt his oet.

_____

**2.** Please wosh me your new shoes.

_____

**3.** nows fell all night long.

_____

**4.** We ate the lewoh pizza.

_____

**5.** Krista bought a loweyl skateboard.

_____

**6.** Scooter dug a lohe in the yard.

_____

**7.** Ming twore a story about a crow.

_____

**8.** Mrs. Sosa egos to lunch with our class.

_____

# More Words with Long o

| | | | |
|---|---|---|---|
| most | hello | over | boat |
| coat | cocoa | comb | both |
| ago | open | toast | road |
| hold | loaf | almost | gold |

**boat**

## Say and Listen

Say each spelling word. Listen for the long o sound.

## Think and Sort

Look at the letters in each word. Think about how long o is spelled. Spell each word aloud.

Long o can be shown as /ō/. How many spelling patterns for /ō/ do you see?

**1.** Write the **ten** spelling words that have the *o* pattern, like *most.*

**2.** Write the **five** spelling words that have the *oa* pattern, like *boat.*

**3.** Write the **one** spelling word that has both the *o* and *oa* patterns.

---

**1. o Words**

_____

_____

_____    **2. oa Words**

_____    _____

_____    _____

_____    _____

_____    _____

_____    **3. o and oa Word**

_____    _____

---

# Definitions

Write the spelling word for each definition.
Use a dictionary if you need to.

**1.** to arrange the hair _____

**2.** a precious metal _____

**3.** in the past _____

**4.** the one as well as the other _____

**5.** a greeting _____

**6.** to keep in the hand _____

**7.** the greatest amount _____

**8.** nearly _____

**9.** to cause something to be no longer closed _____

**10.** above _____

**11.** bread baked in one piece _____

# Classifying

Write the spelling word that belongs in each group.

**12.** hat     scarf     gloves _____

**13.** milk     eggs     cereal _____

**14.** street     avenue     lane _____

**15.** car     train     airplane _____

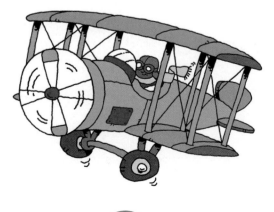

| | | | |
|---|---|---|---|
| most | hello | over | boat |
| coat | cocoa | comb | both |
| ago | open | toast | road |
| hold | loaf | almost | gold |

## Proofreading

Proofread the e-mail below. Use proofreading marks to correct five spelling mistakes, three capitalization mistakes, and two punctuation mistakes.

**Proofreading Marks**

◯ spell correctly

≡ capitalize

? add question mark

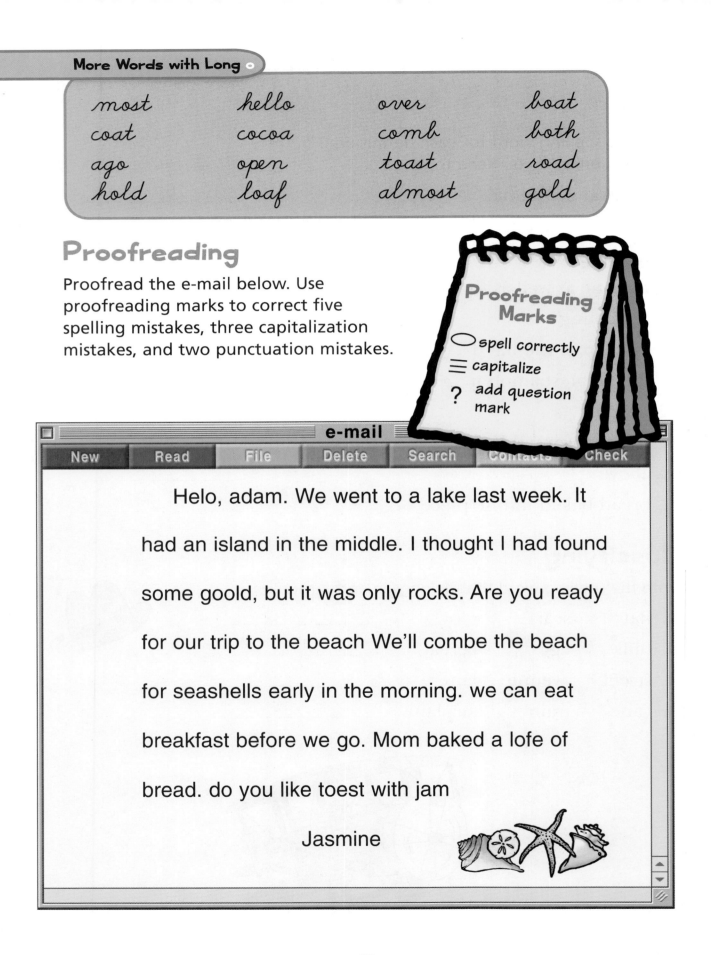

**e-mail**

| New | Read | File | Delete | Search | Contacts | Check |

Helo, adam. We went to a lake last week. It

had an island in the middle. I thought I had found

some goold, but it was only rocks. Are you ready

for our trip to the beach We'll combe the beach

for seashells early in the morning. we can eat

breakfast before we go. Mom baked a lofe of

bread. do you like toest with jam

Jasmine

# Language Connection

## Synonyms

Synonyms are words that have the same meaning.
The words *hello, howdy,* and *hi* are synonyms.

Use spelling words from this lesson to write synonym clues for the puzzle.

### ACROSS

3. _____

4. _____

6. _____

7. _____

### DOWN

1. _____

2. _____

3. _____

5. _____

6. _____

# Words with /o͝o/

| | | | |
|---|---|---|---|
| book | took | cook | sure |
| should | stood | wood | put |
| poor | foot | shook | would |
| full | cookies | pull | could |

cook

## Say and Listen

Say each spelling word. Listen for the vowel sound you hear in *book*.

## Think and Sort

Look at the letters in each word. Think about how the vowel sound in *book* is spelled. Spell each word aloud.

The vowel sound in *book* can be shown as /o͝o/. How many spelling patterns for /o͝o/ do you see?

1. Write the **nine** spelling words that have the *oo* pattern, like *book*.

2. Write the **four** spelling words that have the *u* or *u*-consonant-*e* pattern, like *put*.

3. Write the **three** spelling words that have the *ou* pattern, like *would*.

**1. oo Words**

_____

_____

_____

_____

_____

_____

_____

**2. u, u-consonant-e Words**

_____

_____

_____

_____

**3. ou Words**

_____

_____

_____

## Antonyms

Write the spelling word that is an antonym of each word.

1. push        _____

2. sat        _____

3. uncertain    _____

4. rich        _____

5. empty       _____

6. gave       _____

## Clues

Write the spelling word for each clue.

7. You put a shoe on this part of your body.    _____

8. This word means "ought to."    _____

9. Logs are made of this.    _____

10. Most people like these sweet treats.    _____

11. This word means "was able to."    _____

12. You might do this to prepare food.    _____

13. This word means "to set."    _____

14. This word sounds like *wood*.    _____

15. This word is the past tense of *shake*.    _____

book took cook sure
should stood wood put
poor foot shook would
full cookies pull could

## Proofreading

Proofread the story review below.
Use proofreading marks to correct five
spelling mistakes, three capitalization
mistakes, and two unnecessary words.

Proofreading
Marks

◯ spell correctly
≡ capitalize
ℓ take out

Story Review

The Lion and the Mouse is an an old

story that has stod the test of time. the

beginning will pul you into the story. what

will happen to that that poer little mouse?

Culd the lion be kind enough to let him go?

What lesson does the story teach? If you

have read the story before, then you know.

if not, read it soon. You are shure to enjoy it.

# Language Connection

## Capital Letters

The names of cities and states always begin with a capital letter.

> Phoenix is the capital of Arizona.

Unscramble the spelling words in the sentences below.
Then write the sentences, using capital letters correctly.

1. many dowo products come from maine.

   _____

2. i am rues that the largest state is alaska.

   _____

3. everyone dosluh visit chicago, illinois.

   _____

4. dowlu you like to go to new orleans?

   _____

5. san francisco ohsko during an earthquake.

   _____

6. my friend from toronto sent me some okecois.

   _____

# More Words with -ed or -ing

| | | | |
|---|---|---|---|
| sneezed | smiling | beginning | hoped |
| dropping | shining | stopped | pleased |
| dropped | liked | taking | driving |
| closed | jogged | hopping | shopping |

## Say and Listen

Say the spelling words. Listen for the -ed and -ing endings.

**hopping**

## Think and Sort

Each spelling word is formed by adding -ed or -ing to a base word.
Look at the letters in each spelling word. Spell each word aloud.
Think about how the spelling of the base word changes.

1. If a base word ends in *e*, the *e* is usually dropped before -ed or -ing is added. Write the **nine** spelling words in which the final *e* of the base word is dropped, like *taking*.

2. If a base word ends in a single vowel and a single consonant, the consonant is often doubled before -ed or -ing is added. Write the **seven** spelling words in which the final consonant of the base word is doubled, like *beginning*.

**1. Final e Dropped**

_____

_____

_____

_____

_____

_____

_____

_____

_____

**2. Final Consonant Doubled**

_____

_____

_____

_____

_____

_____

_____

## Synonyms

Write the spelling word that is a synonym for each word.

1. trotted _____
2. starting _____
3. shut _____
4. wished _____
5. enjoyed _____
6. sparkling _____
7. quit _____
8. grinning _____
9. jumping _____

## Rhymes

Write the spelling word that completes each sentence and rhymes with the underlined word.

10. The singer was not <u>pleased</u> when I _____.
11. Are you _____ the cake you are <u>making</u>?
12. The bus <u>stopped</u>, and my backpack _____.
13. To turn <u>diving</u> into _____, add the letter *r*.
14. Mom was not _____ when I <u>teased</u> my brother.
15. I keep _____ the jelly and <u>mopping</u> up the mess.

| | | | |
|---|---|---|---|
| sneezed | smiling | beginning | hoped |
| dropping | shining | stopped | pleased |
| dropped | liked | taking | driving |
| closed | jogged | hopping | shopping |

## Proofreading

Proofread the letter below. Use proofreading marks to correct five spelling mistakes, three capitalization mistakes, and two punctuation mistakes.

**Proofreading Marks**

◯ spell correctly
≡ capitalize
⊙ add period

2616 Lakeview Drive

Gilbert, AZ 85234

May 15, 2004

Dear Tyler,

    Last week we stoped by the animal shelter. i

likd the kittens a lot. my parents said we could

get one I was so pleaseed that I couldn't stop

smilling. when we were driveing home, I thought

of you. Please come see my new kitten soon

        Your friend,

        Samara

## Commas

To make it easy to read a date, use a comma between the day and the year.

July 4, 1776     December 27, 1998

Decide which word from the boxes below completes each sentence.
Then write the sentences, using commas correctly.

jogged     closed     dropped     hoped

1. School ___ for vacation on May 28 2004.

   _____

2. On June 25 1999, Ms. Padden ___ in a race.

   _____

3. Old friends ___ in to visit us on February 4 2003.

   _____

4. Ana ___ her party would be on May 17 2006.

   _____

# unit 4 Review
## Lessons 16-20

**Lesson 16**

socks
bottle
o'clock
wash

### Words with Short o

Write the spelling word that belongs in each group.

1. time, watch, _____
2. jar, can, _____
3. shoes, gloves, _____
4. clean, scrub, _____

**Lesson 17**

wrote
hole
know
yellow
goes
November

### Words with Long o

Write the spelling word for each clue.

5. This is something you might find in your sock. _____
6. If your shirt is the color of butter, it's this color. _____
7. If you recorded your thoughts on paper, you did this. _____
8. Someone who travels does this. _____
9. If you understand, you do this. _____
10. If it's the eleventh month, it's this month. _____

**Lesson 18**

comb
hello
almost
road
toast

### More Words with Long o

Write the spelling word that completes each sentence.

11. Would you like some eggs and _____ for breakfast?
12. The sun was setting, so it was _____ dark outside.

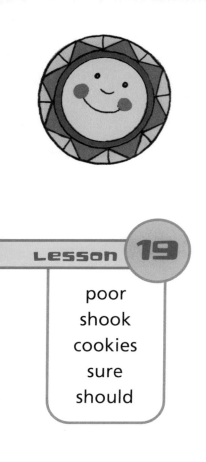

**13.** I use a _____ and a brush to fix my hair.

**14.** This _____ goes all the way to Canada.

**15.** When I see people I know, I say _____ to them.

**Lesson 19**

poor
shook
cookies
sure
should

## Words with /o͝o/

Write the spelling word that completes each analogy.

**16.** *Ice cream* is to *freeze* as _____ is to *bake*.

**17.** *Wake* is to *sleep* as *rich* is to _____.

**18.** *Little* is to *small* as _____ is to *must*.

**19.** *Take* is to *took* as *shake* is to _____.

**20.** *Thin* is to *skinny* as *certain* is to _____.

**Lesson 20**

hoped
shining
stopped
dropped
hopping

## More Words with -ed or -ing

Write the spelling word that is a synonym for each underlined word.

**21.** The stars were <u>glowing</u> like diamonds.

_____

**22.** The temperature <u>fell</u> twenty degrees in three hours. _____

**23.** Cinderella <u>wished</u> she could go to the ball.

_____

**24.** Our washing machine <u>quit</u> working yesterday.

_____

**25.** My little brother was <u>jumping</u> on one foot.

_____

# Words with /o͞o/ or /yo͞o/

| | | | |
|---|---|---|---|
| noon | huge | few | used |
| tooth | blue | school | Tuesday |
| who | knew | two | true |
| too | news | move | June |

**huge**

## Say and Listen

Say each spelling word. Listen for the vowel sound you hear in *noon* and *huge*.

## Think and Sort

The vowel sound in *noon* and *huge* can be shown as /o͞o/. In *huge* and some other /o͞o/ words, *y* is pronounced before /o͞o/.

Look at the letters in each word. Think about how /o͞o/ or /yo͞o/ is spelled. Spell each word aloud.

1. Write the **four** spelling words with the *oo* pattern, like *noon*.

2. Write the **six** spelling words with the *ue* or *ew* pattern, like *true*.

3. Write the **three** spelling words with the *u*-consonant-*e* pattern, like *huge*.

4. Write the **three** spelling words with the *o* or *o*-consonant-*e* pattern, like *move*.

**1. oo Words**

_____    _____

_____    _____

_____    **3. u-consonant-e Words**

_____    _____

**2. ue, ew Words**    _____

_____    _____

_____    **4. o, o-consonant-e Words**

_____    _____

_____    _____

_____

# Classifying

Write the spelling word that belongs in each group.

1. lunch time   twelve o'clock   _____
2. report   information   _____
3. what   where   _____
4. mouth   tongue   _____
5. wiggle   walk   _____
6. post office   library   _____
7. red   green   _____

# Clues

Write the spelling word for each clue.

8. one of the summer months   _____
9. not very many   _____
10. the sum of one plus one   _____
11. means the same as *also*   _____
12. gigantic   _____
13. the opposite of *false*   _____
14. not new   _____
15. sounds like *new*   _____

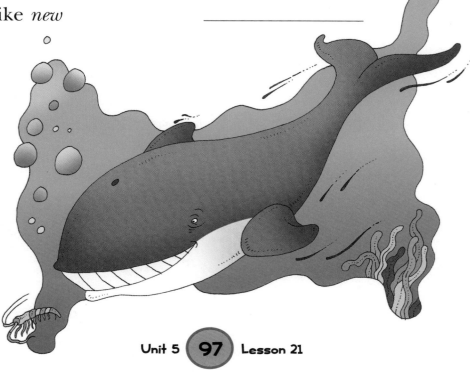

| | | | |
|---|---|---|---|
| noon | huge | few | used |
| tooth | blue | school | Tuesday |
| who | knew | two | true |
| too | news | move | June |

## Proofreading

Proofread the journal entry below. Use proofreading marks to correct five spelling mistakes, three capitalization mistakes, and two punctuation mistakes.

**Proofreading Marks**

◯ spell correctly
≡ capitalize
⊙ add period

June 2

here is the big news for the week. On Toosday I ran in a race at the school track it started at nune and was tue miles long. I wore my green and bloo shirt. Lots of people ran in the race There were adults, children, and grandparents. Uncle Scott came with Mom to see me run. guess whue won. I did!

# Dictionary Skills

## Pronunciation

Most dictionary entries show how a word is said.
The way a word is said is called its pronunciation.

Entry Word ⟶ **noon** (nōōn) *noun* Midday; 12 o'clock in the middle of the day: *We'll eat at noon.*

Pronunciation

Letters and symbols are used to write pronunciations. These letters and symbols can be found in the pronunciation key.

### Pronunciation Key

| | | | | | |
|---|---|---|---|---|---|
| ă | pat | îr | deer | *th* | this |
| ā | pay | ŏ | pot | ŭ | cut |
| âr | care | ō | toe | ûr | urge |
| ä | father | ô | paw, for | ə | about, |
| ĕ | pet | oi | noise | | item, |
| ē | bee | ŏŏ | took | | edible, |
| ĭ | pit | ōō | boot | | gallop, |
| ī | pie | ou | out | | circus |
| | | th | thin | | |

Use the pronunciation key to write the word from the boxes that goes with each pronunciation. Check your answers in the dictionary.

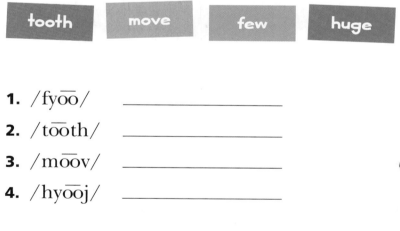

**tooth**　　**move**　　**few**　　**huge**

**1.** /fyōo/ _____

**2.** /tōoth/ _____

**3.** /mōov/ _____

**4.** /hyōoj/ _____

# Words with /ûr/

| | | | |
|---|---|---|---|
| curl | world | learn | turn |
| were | girl | word | bird |
| work | earth | first | Thursday |
| dirt | worm | fur | third |

**bird**

## Say and Listen

The spelling words for this lesson contain the /ûr/ sound you hear in *curl*. Say each spelling word. Listen for the /ûr/ sound.

## Think and Sort

Look at the letters in each word. Think about how the /ûr/ sounds are spelled. Spell each word aloud. How many spelling patterns for /ûr/ do you see?

1.  Write the **four** spelling words that have the *ur* pattern, like *curl*.

2.  Write the **five** spelling words that have the *ir* pattern, like *first*.

3.  Write the **four** spelling words that have the *or* pattern, like *work*.

4.  Write the **two** spelling words that have the *ear* pattern, like *earth*.

5.  Write the **one** spelling word that has the *ere* pattern.

**1. ur Words**

_____

_____

_____

_____

**2. ir Words**

_____

_____

_____

_____

_____

**3. or Words**

_____

_____

_____

_____

**4. ear Words**

_____

_____

**5. ere Word**

_____

# Definitions

Write the spelling word for each definition.
Use a dictionary if you need to.

1. a long, thin creature that crawls _____

2. a young female child _____

3. the third planet from the sun _____

4. coming at the beginning _____

5. next after second _____

6. to move around _____

7. the day between Wednesday and Friday _____

8. a group of letters that has a meaning _____

9. soil or earth _____

# Synonyms

Write the spelling word that is a synonym for the
underlined word in each sentence.

10. Dinosaurs <u>existed</u> on Earth long ago. _____

11. Next year I hope to <u>study</u> French. _____

12. We finished our <u>task</u> in the garden. _____

13. I will <u>loop</u> my hair around my finger. _____

14. Wouldn't it be fun to go around the <u>earth</u>? _____

15. Our dog's <u>hair</u> is thick and black. _____

| curl | world | learn | turn |
| were | girl | word | bird |
| work | earth | first | Thursday |
| dirt | worm | fur | third |

## Proofreading

Proofread this paragraph from a story. Use proofreading marks to correct five spelling mistakes, three capitalization mistakes, and two punctuation mistakes.

**Proofreading Marks**

◯ spell correctly
≡ capitalize
⊙ add period

Four young robins fluttered to the ground. The first bird ate a werm. the second one ate a bug. The therd bird said bugs made his feathers kurl. he saw a berry in the dert and ate it The fourth bird had work to do. For an hour she dug in the erth. the fifth bird slept late that morning He said it was his day off!

## Language Connection

### Synonyms and Antonyms

Synonyms are words that have the same meaning.
Antonyms are words that have opposite meanings.

small    little          thick    thin

Write the word from the boxes below that is an antonym
of each word.

dirty     add     huge     young

**1.** subtract _____

**2.** clean _____

**3.** tiny _____

**4.** old _____

Each group of four words below has a pair of antonyms and a pair
of synonyms. First write the antonyms. Then write the synonyms.

full     turn     empty     spin

**5.** Antonyms _____

**6.** Synonyms _____

earth     first     world     last

**7.** Antonyms _____

**8.** Synonyms _____

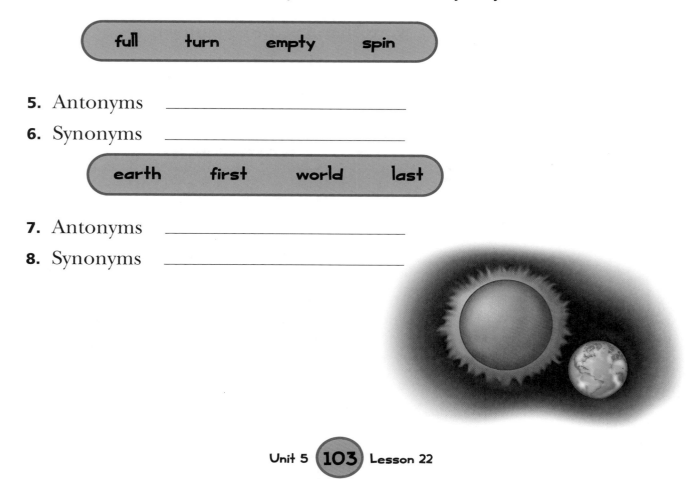

# Words with /ä/

| | | | |
|---|---|---|---|
| dark | yard | art | market |
| garden | hard | heart | father |
| March | arm | barn | start |
| star | card | sharp | bark |

**garden**

## Say and Listen

Say each spelling word. Listen for the vowel sound you hear in *dark*.

## Think and Sort

Look at the letters in each word. Think about how the vowel sound in *dark* is spelled. Spell each word aloud.

The vowel sound in *dark* can be shown as /ä/. How many spelling patterns for /ä/ do you see?

**1.** Write the **fifteen** spelling words that have the *a* pattern, like *dark*.

**2.** Write the **one** spelling word that has the *ea* pattern.

**1. a Words**

_____     _____

_____     _____

_____     _____

_____     _____

_____     _____

_____     **2. ea Word**

_____     _____

_____

# Clues

Write the spelling word for each clue.

1. where flowers grow _____

2. where to buy fruits and vegetables _____

3. month after February _____

4. what you send on someone's birthday _____

5. where farm animals sleep _____

6. a place to play near a house _____

7. what the inside of a cave is _____

8. what stones are _____

9. another word for *dad* _____

10. the kind of knife you need to cut things _____

11. what the car does when Mom turns the key _____

12. a drawing or painting _____

# Multiple Meanings

Write the spelling word that has more than one meaning
and completes each sentence below.

13. The movie _____ wished upon a shining _____.

14. My _____ pounded as I put all my _____
into the final leg of the race.

15. I heard Scooter _____ at the squirrel gnawing on the
tree _____.

| | | | |
|---|---|---|---|
| dark | yard | art | market |
| garden | hard | heart | father |
| March | arm | barn | start |
| star | card | sharp | bark |

## Proofreading

Proofread the announcement below. Use proofreading marks to correct five spelling mistakes, three capitalization mistakes, and two punctuation mistakes.

Proofreading Marks

◯ spell correctly
≡ capitalize
? add question mark

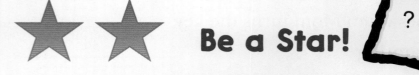

**Be a Star!**

Do you dance or sing Can you do carde tricks?

are you good at aret? The Near North neighbors

are having a talent show. We will steart practicing

next week. we also need someone to paint signs.

The show will end with a parade around the Near

North Park flower gardin. Would you like to join

us Come to mary Wu's yarde on Friday after

school!

# Dictionary Skills

## Multiple Meanings

Some words have more than one meaning. Look at this entry for *heart*. The word *heart* has two meanings. Each is numbered. Read the sample sentence for each meaning of *heart*. The words around the word *heart* give a clue to its meaning.

> **heart** (härt) *noun, plural* **hearts**
> **1.** The organ in the chest that pumps blood through the body: *The doctor listened to my heart.* **2.** Courage and enthusiasm: *He put his heart into winning the game.*

Write **Meaning 1** or **Meaning 2** to indicate which definition of *heart* is used in each sentence. Then write your own sentences showing you understand each meaning of *heart*.

1. Our class lost **heart** when we lost the game. _____

2. My **heart** beats fast after a race. _____

_____

_____

# Words with /oi/

| | | | |
|---|---|---|---|
| coin | boy | choice | spoil |
| royal | boil | voice | toy |
| soil | joy | noise | point |
| broil | enjoy | join | oil |

**boy**

## Say and Listen

Say each spelling word. Listen for the vowel sound you hear in *coin*.

## Think and Sort

Look at the letters in each word. Think about how the vowel sound in *coin* is spelled. Spell each word aloud.

The vowel sound in *coin* can be shown as /oi/. How many spelling patterns for /oi/ do you see?

**1.** Write the **eleven** spelling words that have the *oi* pattern, like *coin*.

**2.** Write the **five** spelling words that have the *oy* pattern, like *toy*.

**1. oi** Words

_____      _____

_____      _____

_____      **2. oy** Words

_____      _____

_____      _____

_____      _____

_____      _____

_____

# Classifying

Write the spelling word that belongs in each group of words.

1. noble      kingly      _____
2. gas      coal      _____
3. doll      yo-yo      _____
4. happiness      pleasure      _____
5. sound      speech      _____
6. rot      decay      _____
7. tie      connect      _____
8. money      dollar bill      _____

# Analogies

Write the spelling word that completes each analogy.

9. *Man* is to *woman* as _____ is to *girl*.
10. *Laugh* is to _____ as *cry* is to *fear*.
11. *Lose* is to *loss* as *choose* is to _____.
12. *Soft* is to *whisper* as *loud* is to _____.
13. *Ocean* is to *sea* as _____ is to *dirt*.
14. *Cake* is to *bake* as *steak* is to _____.
15. *Finger* is to _____ as *hand* is to *wave*.

| | | | |
|---|---|---|---|
| coin | boy | choice | spoil |
| royal | boil | voice | toy |
| soil | joy | noise | point |
| broil | enjoy | join | oil |

## Proofreading

Proofread the e-mail below.
Use proofreading marks to correct
five spelling mistakes, three capitalization
mistakes, and two punctuation mistakes.

### Proofreading Marks

⬯ spell correctly
≡ capitalize
⊙ add period

**e-mail**

| New | Read | File | Delete | Search |
|---|---|---|---|---|

Diego,

Last night I dreamed I lived in a royle castle. I had

every toy a boy could want What I had for breakfast,

lunch, and dinner was my choic. nothing could spoyal

my joi Then I heard a noise. It was the voyce of my

brother, james. It was so loud that it woke me up.

Have you ever had a dream like this? I would enjoy

reading about it. send me an e-mail.

Tomas

## Capital Letters

The following kinds of words begin with a capital letter:

- **the first word of a sentence**
- **the names of streets**
- **the names of people and pets**
- **the names of cities and states**

Write each sentence below, using capital letters correctly.
Circle the spelling word in the sentence.

**1.** we will enjoy visiting minneapolis.

_____

**2.** my dog max makes a lot of noise!

_____

**3.** can you point out mallory street?

_____

**4.** this coin was made in colorado.

_____

**5.** mrs. hays bought a toy for her baby.

_____

**6.** kevin and I want to join the baseball team.

_____

# More Contractions

| | | | |
|---|---|---|---|
| isn't | weren't | can't | doesn't |
| hadn't | mustn't | wouldn't | won't |
| shouldn't | aren't | wasn't | don't |
| couldn't | didn't | hasn't | haven't |

won't

## Say and Listen

Say the spelling words. Listen for the sounds at the end of each word.

## Think and Sort

All of the spelling words in this lesson are contractions. Each contraction is formed from the word *not* joined with another word. When the two words are joined, one or more letters are left out. An apostrophe ( ' ) is used to show the missing letters.

In the contraction *won't*, the spelling of *will* changes to *wo*. One contraction, *can't*, is formed from one word, not two separate words.

1. Write the **fifteen** spelling words that are formed from *not* joined with a separate word, like *isn't*.

2. Write the **one** spelling word that is formed from one word.

**1.** Two Words

_____        _____

_____        _____

_____        _____

_____        _____

_____        **2.** One Word

_____        _____

_____

## Either . . . or

Write the spelling word that completes each sentence.

1. Either Wags will or he _____.
2. Either you do or you _____.
3. Either James could or he _____.
4. Either Julie would or she _____.
5. Either Sara does or she _____.
6. Either Ricky was or he _____.

## Trading Places

Write the contraction that can be used instead of the underlined word or words in each sentence.

7. Marta <u>had not</u> seen the new puppy.          _____
8. You <u>must not</u> touch the wet paint.          _____
9. Lan <u>did not</u> bring his lunch.          _____
10. I <u>cannot</u> believe you ran five miles!          _____
11. The mail <u>has not</u> come yet.          _____
12. I <u>have not</u> finished my homework.          _____
13. Did you know that whales <u>are not</u> fish?          _____
14. We <u>were not</u> home on Saturday.          _____
15. "That <u>is not</u> my car," Ms. Ford said.          _____

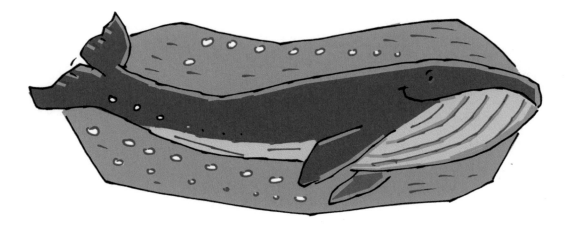

## More Contractions

| | | | |
|---|---|---|---|
| *isn't* | *weren't* | *can't* | *doesn't* |
| *hadn't* | *mustn't* | *wouldn't* | *won't* |
| *shouldn't* | *aren't* | *wasn't* | *don't* |
| *couldn't* | *didn't* | *hasn't* | *haven't* |

## Proofreading

Proofread the note below. Use proofreading marks to correct five spelling mistakes, three capitalization mistakes, and two unnecessary words.

**Proofreading Marks**

◯ spell correctly
≡ capitalize
ℓ take out

Chad,

   I couldnt' wait for you to see this game.

Open the box and look at the checkerboard. it

has'nt been used in in ten years. It's still in great

shape! Wouldent you like to play? Well, Aunt rose

won'nt let anyone use it except me and one other

person. you are that person. I'll come to your

house tonight for a game. Doesnt' that sound like

like a great plan?

                              Ling

## Be Verbs

There are many different forms of the verb *be*. Some tell what is happening now. Others tell what happened in the past. These forms of *be* are used in *not* contractions.

| Present Tense | | Contraction |
|---|---|---|
| is | The bus **is** late. | isn't |
| are | They **are** in a hurry. | aren't |

| Past Tense | | Contraction |
|---|---|---|
| was | Bart **was** still here. | wasn't |
| were | Jill and Will **were** on the way. | weren't |

Use the correct contraction above to complete each sentence.

**1.** Toni _____ here every day.

**2.** Today the trains _____ on time.

**3.** Paige and Wanda _____ here last Thursday.

**4.** Last month _____ the best month for planting a garden.

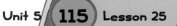

# unit 5 Review
## Lessons 21-25

### Words with /o͞o/ or /yo͞o/

too
true
knew
few
huge
used
two

Write the spelling word that can be used instead of the word or words in dark type in each sentence.

1. The story that we read was **real**. _____

2. My father's car is **not new**. _____

3. The sun is **very** hot in the summer. _____

4. **One plus one** is less than three. _____

5. Malika **was certain** that she would win. _____

6. **Not very many** people stood in line. _____

7. Elephants and whales are **big**. _____

### Words with /ûr/

curl
girl
worm
earth
were

Write the spelling word that belongs in each group.

8. lady      woman      _____

9. are       was        _____

10. curve    coil       _____

11. soil     ground     _____

12. snake    eel        _____

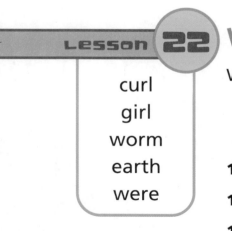

## LESSON 23

garden
father
sharp
heart

# Words with /ä/

Write the spelling word that completes each analogy.

**13.** *Scissors* is to _____ as *feather* is to *soft*.

**14.** *Son* is to _____ as *daughter* is to *mother*.

**15.** *Apple* is to *orchard* as *carrot* is to _____.

**16.** *Brain* is to *head* as _____ is to *chest*.

## LESSON 24

voice
soil
enjoy
royal

# Words with /oi/

Write the spelling word for each clue.

**17.** People sing with this. _____

**18.** This is a synonym for *like*.

_____

**19.** Kings and queens are this.

_____

**20.** People plant seeds in this.

_____

## LESSON 25

weren't
won't
aren't
haven't
can't

# More Contractions

Write the contractions for the words.

**21.** cannot _____

**22.** are + not _____

**23.** have + not _____

**24.** will + not _____

**25.** were + not _____

## Words with /ô/

| | | | |
|---|---|---|---|
| draw | walk | bought | because |
| frog | along | long | water |
| always | brought | off | belong |
| mall | strong | tall | talk |

**strong**

## Say and Listen

Say each spelling word. Listen for the vowel sound you hear in *draw*.

## Think and Sort

Look at the letters in each word. Think about how the vowel sound in *draw* is spelled. Spell each word aloud.

The vowel sound in *draw* can be shown as /ô/. How many spelling patterns for /ô/ do you see?

1. Write the **six** spelling words that have the *o* pattern, like *long*.

2. Write the **six** spelling words that have the *a* pattern, like *talk*.

3. Write the **two** spelling words that have the *ough* pattern, like *bought*.

4. Write the **one** spelling word that has the *au* pattern.

5. Write the **one** spelling word that has the *aw* pattern.

**1. o Words**

_____     _____

_____     _____

_____     **3. ough Words**

_____     _____

_____     _____

**2. a Words**     **4. au Word**

_____     _____

_____     **5. aw Word**

_____     _____

## Antonyms

Write the spelling word that is an antonym of each underlined word.

1. That basketball player is very <u>short</u>. _____
2. Please turn <u>on</u> the light. _____
3. Tina <u>never</u> eats breakfast. _____
4. Elephants are very large and <u>weak</u>. _____
5. Mr. Good gave a <u>brief</u> speech. _____

## Clues

Write the spelling word for each clue.

6. what you do on the phone _____
7. what people and animals drink _____
8. place to shop _____
9. past tense of bring _____
10. what artists do _____
11. green thing that sits on a lily pad _____
12. means "to be owned by" _____
13. means almost the same as *beside* _____
14. rhymes with *talk* _____
15. past tense of *buy* _____

*draw* *walk* *bought* *because*
*frog* *along* *long* *water*
*always* *brought* *off* *belong*
*mall* *strong* *tall* *talk*

## Proofreading

Proofread the e-mail below. Use proofreading marks to correct five spelling mistakes, four capitalization mistakes, and two unnecessary words.

**Proofreading Marks**

○ spell correctly
≡ capitalize
ℓ take out

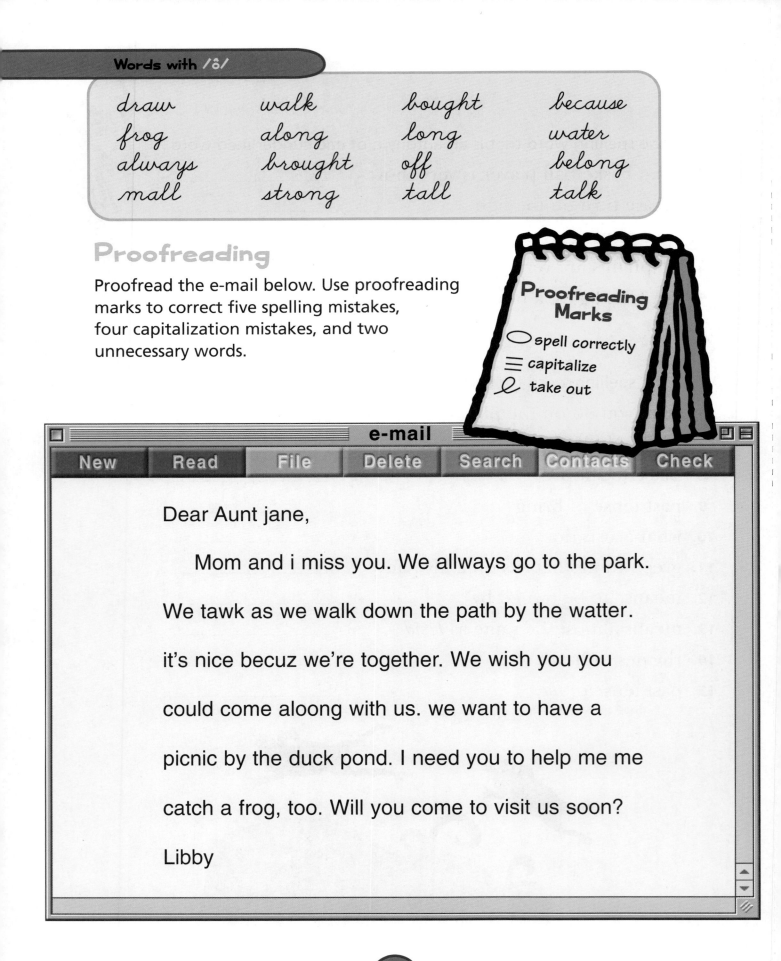

**e-mail**

| New | Read | File | Delete | Search | Contacts | Check |

Dear Aunt jane,

Mom and i miss you. We allways go to the park.

We tawk as we walk down the path by the watter.

it's nice becuz we're together. We wish you you

could come aloong with us. we want to have a

picnic by the duck pond. I need you to help me me

catch a frog, too. Will you come to visit us soon?

Libby

### Subject and Predicate

The subject of a sentence tells who or what is doing the action or being talked about. The predicate of a sentence tells what the subject does or did.

| Subject | Predicate |
|---------|-----------|
| Sally | danced. |
| The cat | had jumped off the chair. |

Unscramble the spelling words as you write the sentences below. Then circle the subjects and underline the predicates.

**1.** My sister hid behind a latl tree.

_____

**2.** Ling tughob a baseball.

_____

**3.** Mrs. Martinez took a nogl vacation.

_____

**4.** I will wrad a picture of you.

_____

**5.** The old clock fell fof the shelf.

_____

# More Words with /ô/

| | | | |
|---|---|---|---|
| August | morning | four | quart |
| pour | popcorn | before | autumn |
| corner | storm | door | floor |
| north | born | fork | sport |

**popcorn**

## Say and Listen

Say each spelling word. Listen for the first vowel sound you hear in *August* and *morning*.

## Think and Sort

Look at the letters in each word. Think about how the first vowel sound in *August* and *morning* is spelled. Spell each word aloud.

The first vowel sound in *August* and *morning* can be shown as /ô/. How many spelling patterns for /ô/ do you see?

1. Write the **two** spelling words that have the *au* pattern, like *August*.

2. Write the **nine** spelling words that have the *o* pattern, like *morning*.

3. Write the **four** spelling words that have the *oo* or *ou* pattern, like *door*.

4. Write the **one** spelling word that has the *a* pattern.

**1. au Words**

_____     _____

_____     _____

**2. o Words**                  **3. oo, ou Words**

_____     _____

_____     _____

_____     _____

_____     _____

_____     **4. a Word**

_____     _____

## Clues

Write the spelling word for each clue.

1. snack to eat at the movies             _____

2. spoon, knife, _____             _____

3. rain or snow and lots of wind      _____

4. where the walls in a room meet     _____

5. how to get milk into a glass      _____

## Analogies

Write the spelling word that completes each analogy.

6. *East* is to *west* as _____ is to *south*.

7. *Summer* is to *winter* as *spring* is to _____.

8. *Evening* is to *dinner* as _____ is to *breakfast*.

9. *Cool* is to *warm* as *after* is to _____.

10. *Foot* is to *yard* as _____ is to *gallon*.

11. *Above* is to *below* as *ceiling* is to _____.

12. *Lid* is to *jar* as _____ is to *house*.

13. *One* is to *two* as *three* is to _____.

14. *Color* is to *blue* as _____ is to *hockey*.

15. *Bird* is to *hatched* as *child* is to _____.

August    morning    four    quart
pour      popcorn    before  autumn
corner    storm      door    floor
north     born       fork    sport

## Proofreading

Proofread the paragraph below. Use proofreading marks to correct five spelling mistakes, three capitalization mistakes, and two punctuation mistakes.

**Proofreading Marks**
○ spell correctly
≡ capitalize
⊙ add period

Hiking is a great spoort. It can be a lot of fun. here are some things to remember when you go Make sure you are wearing good shoes. Befour you go, put water and snacks in a backpack Trail mix and popcawrn are good snacks. also, bring rain gear in case there is a stourm. It's a good idea to start early in the morening, when you have lots of energy. As you hike along, remember to stop and rest. you will have more fun if you don't get too tired.

## Dictionary Skills

## Alphabetical Order

Many words begin with the same letter or the same two letters. To put these words in alphabetical order, use the third letter of each word. Look at the two words below.

tr in     tr m

Both words start with the letters *tr*. To put them in alphabetical order, look at the third letter. The third letter in *train* is *a*. The third letter in *trim* is *i*. In the alphabet, *a* comes before *i*, so *train* comes before *trim*.

In each list below, the words begin with the same two letters. Look at the third letter of each word. Then write the words in alphabetical order.

**1.** autumn   aunt   August

_____

_____

_____

**2.** porch   point   pour

_____

_____

_____

**3.** fond   four   foggy

_____

_____

_____

**4.** money   morning   moon

_____

_____

_____

# Words with /ou/

| | | | |
|---|---|---|---|
| house | flower | town | sound |
| ground | tower | found | brown |
| about | hour | power | down |
| around | count | our | owl |

**house**

## Say and Listen

Say each spelling word. Listen for the vowel sound you hear in *house*.

## Think and Sort

Look at the letters in each word. Think about how the vowel sound in *house* is spelled. Spell each word aloud.

The vowel sound in *house* can be shown as /ou/. How many spelling patterns for /ou/ do you see?

1. Write the **nine** spelling words that have the *ou* pattern, like *house*.

2. Write the **seven** spelling words that have the *ow* pattern, like *brown*.

**1. ou Words**

_____

_____

_____

_____

_____

_____

_____

_____

_____

**2. ow Words**

_____

_____

_____

_____

_____

_____

_____

# Hink Pinks

Hink pinks are pairs of rhyming words that have funny meanings.
Read each clue. Write the spelling word that completes each
hink pink.

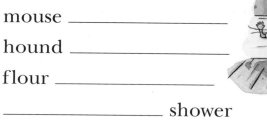

1. a place for mice to live     mouse _____
2. a beagle's bark     hound _____
3. the time to bake     flour _____
4. rain falling on a tall building     _____ shower
5. a night bird's loud sound     _____ howl

# Letter Scramble

Unscramble the letters in parentheses.
Then write the spelling word to complete the phrase.

6. (wodn)     run _____ the hill
7. (repow)     _____ from electricity
8. (boaut)     books for and _____ children
9. (wolfer)     a _____ in a vase
10. (ungord)     on the _____ or in the air
11. (dnofu)     lost and _____
12. (nuoct)     _____ to ten
13. (wonrb)     _____ hair and eyes
14. (ruodna)     in, _____, and through
15. (rou)     her, their, and _____

| | | | |
|---|---|---|---|
| house | flower | town | sound |
| ground | tower | found | brown |
| about | hour | power | down |
| around | count | our | owl |

## Proofreading

Proofread the journal entry below. Use proofreading marks to correct five spelling mistakes, three capitalization mistakes, and two unnecessary words.

**Proofreading Marks**

◯ spell correctly
≡ capitalize
ℓ take out

May 14

    Today was a wild day! Dad and I heard a strange sownd. we looked around the inside of the howse. Then we looked outside. Finally we climbed up on the roof. We found an owel stuck in our our chimney. Dad got his gloves and a fishing net. it took us an hour to free the big broun bird, but it seemed all right as it flew away. I can't wait to to tell chris abuot it.

# Dictionary Skills

## Using the Spelling Table

A spelling table can help you find the spelling of a word in a dictionary. Suppose you are not sure how the vowel sound in *should* is spelled. You can use a spelling table to find the different spellings for the sound. First, find the pronunciation symbol for the sound. Then read the first spelling listed for /o͝o/ and look up *shoold* in a dictionary. Look for each spelling in the dictionary until you find the correct one.

| Sound | Spellings | Examples |
|-------|-----------|----------|
| /o͝o/ | oo  ou  u  u_e | book, could, pull, sure |

Write the correct spelling for each word. Use the Spelling Table on page 141 and a dictionary. One word has two correct spellings.

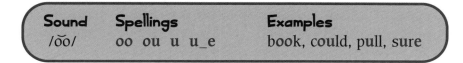

1. /brôth/     _____

2. /mān **tān'**/     _____

3. /ăd **mīr'**/     _____

4. /dōm/     _____

5. /fīr/     _____

6. /wīr/     _____

7. /stärch/     _____

8. /dîr/     _____    _____

# Words with /îr/, /âr/, or /īr/

| | | | |
|---|---|---|---|
| near | care | fire | where |
| hear | wire | stairs | deer |
| ear | year | tire | here |
| dear | chair | air | hair |

**fire**

## Say and Listen

The spelling words for this lesson contain the /îr/, /âr/, and /īr/ sounds that you hear in *near*, *care*, and *fire*. Say the spelling words. Listen for the /îr/, /âr/, and /īr/ sounds.

## Think and Sort

Look at the letters in each word. Think about how the /îr/, /âr/, or /īr/ sounds are spelled. Spell each word aloud.

1. Write the **seven** /îr/ spelling words, like *deer*. Circle the letters that spell /îr/ in each word.

2. Write the **six** /âr/ spelling words, like *care*. Circle the letters that spell /âr/ in each word.

3. Write the **three** /īr/ spelling words, like *fire*. Circle the letters that spell /īr/ in each word.

**1. /îr/ Words**

_____    _____

_____    _____

_____    _____

_____    _____

_____    **3. /īr/ Words**

_____    _____

**2. /âr/ Words**    _____

_____    _____

## Synonyms

Write the spelling word that is a synonym of the underlined word.

1. Look at the long <u>fur</u> on that dog! _____

2. These <u>steps</u> go to the attic. _____

3. Don't trip over that <u>cord</u>. _____

4. The Rileys are <u>loved</u> family friends. _____

## Clues

Write the spelling word for each clue.

5. You breathe this. _____

6. This animal can have antlers. _____

7. When you listen, you do this. _____

8. If you are concerned, you do this. _____

9. You hear with this. _____

10. This equals 12 months. _____

11. This means the opposite of *far*. _____

12. This is a question word. _____

13. A car should have a spare one. _____

14. Matches can start this. _____

15. This means the opposite of *there*. _____

| | | | |
|---|---|---|---|
| near | care | fire | where |
| hear | wire | stairs | deer |
| ear | year | tire | here |
| dear | chair | air | hair |

## Proofreading

Proofread the ad for a Cozy Quilt below. Use proofreading marks to correct five spelling mistakes, three capitalization mistakes, and two punctuation mistakes.

**Proofreading Marks**

◯ spell correctly
≡ capitalize
? add question mark

Cozy Quilt

are you toasty warm on cold winter nights If not, try a Cozy Quilt. do you like to curl up in a chare and read So do I! With a Cozy Quilt, I don't have to sit nere the fire. The aire outside may be cold, but i don't caire. Even on the coldest night of the yeer, my Cozy Quilt keeps me as snug as a bug in a rug!

# Dictionary Skills

## Pronunciation

Letters and symbols are used to write pronunciations in a dictionary. The letters and symbols can be found in the pronunciation key.

| Pronunciation Key | | | | | |
|---|---|---|---|---|---|
| ă  pat | ĕ  pet | îr  deer | oi  noise | th  thin | ə  about, |
| ā  pay | ē  bee | ŏ  pot | o͝o  took | th  this | item, |
| âr  care | ĭ  pit | ō  toe | o͞o  boot | ŭ  cut | edible, |
| ä  father | ī  pie | ô  paw, for | ou  out | ûr  urge | gallop, |
| | | | | | circus |

Write the three words from the boxes that go with each pronunciation.

stairs   wire   where   here   near

fire   year   tire   hair

**1.** /âr/ _____  _____  _____

**2.** /ī r/ _____  _____  _____

**3.** /îr/ _____  _____  _____

# Words with -er or -est

| | | | |
|---|---|---|---|
| taller | tallest | longer | longest |
| dirtier | dirtiest | hotter | hottest |
| stronger | strongest | greater | greatest |
| funnier | funniest | sharper | sharpest |

**taller**

## Say and Listen

Say each spelling word. Listen for the ending sounds.

## Think and Sort

All of the spelling words end in *-er* or *-est*. Spell each word aloud.

Each spelling word is formed by adding *-er* or *-est* to a base word.
Look at the letters of each base word.

1. Write the **ten** spelling words that have no change in the base word, like *taller*.

2. Write the **four** spelling words in which the final *y* of the base word is changed to *i*, like *funnier*.

3. Write the **two** spelling words in which the final consonant of the base word is doubled, like *hotter*.

---

**1. No Change to Base Word**

_____

_____

_____

_____

_____

_____

_____

**2. Final y Changed to i**

_____

_____

_____

_____

**3. Final Consonant Doubled**

_____

_____

## Antonyms

Write the spelling word that is an antonym
of the underlined word.

1. Turn on the fan if it gets <u>colder</u>. _____

2. I need the <u>dullest</u> knife for the steak. _____

3. An owl's eyes are <u>duller</u> than a robin's. _____

4. The <u>weakest</u> wrestler is most likely to win. _____

5. I will put the <u>cleanest</u> clothes in the wash. _____

## Comparisons

Write the spelling word that completes each comparison.

6. An oak tree is _____ than a person.

7. Her joke was the _____ one I ever heard.

8. Mt. Everest is the _____ mountain in the world.

9. Four is _____ than three.

10. A mile is _____ than a foot.

11. An elephant is _____ than a mouse.

12. The Nile River is the _____ river in the world.

13. Summer is usually the _____ season of the year.

14. Who is the _____ basketball player of all time?

15. I thought the joke was _____ than the riddle.

*taller     tallest     longer     longest*
*dirtier     dirtiest     hotter     hottest*
*stronger     strongest     greater     greatest*
*funnier     funniest     sharper     sharpest*

## Proofreading

Proofread this paragraph from a newspaper article. Use proofreading marks to correct five spelling mistakes, three capitalization mistakes, and two punctuation mistakes.

**Proofreading Marks**

◯ spell correctly
≡ capitalize
⊙ add period

### Gabby's Garden Tips

spring is the greatist season of them all The sun shines stronger than in winter. The days are longger. the trees and grass grow taler and faster. Early spring is the time to start a flower garden Digging in the earth might make your hands dirtyer than watching TV, but it will also make you happier! A flower garden is something everyone can enjoy. having lots of bright, colorful flowers will make your spring even grater !

## Adjectives

An adjective describes a noun or a pronoun. It tells which, what kind, or how many.

> The strong man lifted the box.    Mike is strong.

Add *-er* to most adjectives to compare two people or things.
Add *-est* to compare more than two people or things.

> Cliff is stronger than Mike.    Paul is the strongest of all.

Use the correct word from the boxes to write each sentence.

greater    hotter    funniest    tallest

**1.** Sharon tells the ___ jokes we've ever heard.

_____

**2.** The sun is ___ today than it was yesterday.

_____

**3.** Gigi is the ___ girl on the basketball team.

_____

**4.** Twenty is ___ than ten.

_____

# unit 6 Review
## Lessons 26-30

LESSON **26**

strong
talk
bought
because
draw

## Words with /ô/

Unscramble the letters in parentheses. Then write the spelling word to complete the sentence.

1. (thobug) Maria _____ two tickets to the concert.

2. (abesceu) We could not see _____ of the tall post.

3. (torsgn) That horse has very _____ legs.

4. (kalt) Let's _____ about the game.

5. (ward) Can you _____ a picture of the house?

LESSON **27**

autumn
before
floor
pour
quart

## More Words with /ô/

Write the spelling word for each clue.

6. This is a measure for liquids.

   _____

7. You do this with water in a pitcher.

   _____

8. This season comes before winter.

   _____

9. This word is the opposite of *after*.

   _____

10. This can be covered with tile or carpet.

   _____

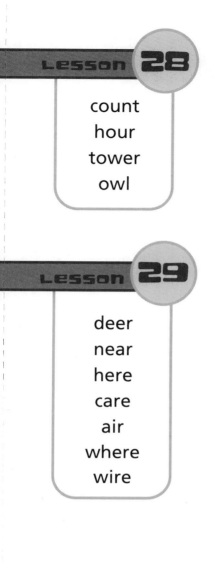

## LESSON 28

count
hour
tower
owl

## Words with /ou/

Write the spelling word that completes each analogy.

**11.** *Days* is to *week* as *minutes* is to _____.

**12.** *Terrier* is to *dog* as _____ is to *bird*.

**13.** *Read* is to *book* as _____ is to *money*.

**14.** *House* is to *garage* as *castle* is to _____.

## LESSON 29

deer
near
here
care
air
where
wire

## Words with /îr/, /âr/, or /ir/

Write the spelling word that completes each sentence.

**15.** The smell of lilacs filled the _____.

**16.** The _____ darted across the road.

**17.** Do you know _____ my keys are?

**18.** We can rest _____ in the shade.

**19.** The cage was made of wood and _____.

**20.** Our hotel is _____ the park.

**21.** Heidi takes good _____ of her pet.

## LESSON 30

greater
sharpest
funnier
hottest

## Words with -er or -est

Write the spelling word that belongs in each group.

**22.** sharp        sharper        _____

**23.** great        _____        greatest

**24.** hot        hotter        _____

**25.** funny        _____        funniest

# commonly misspelled words

| | | | |
|---|---|---|---|
| about | family | name | that's |
| above | favorite | nice | their |
| across | finally | now | then |
| again | friend | once | there |
| a lot | friends | one | they |
| always | from | our | though |
| another | get | out | today |
| baby | getting | outside | too |
| because | girl | party | two |
| been | goes | people | upon |
| before | guess | play | very |
| beginning | have | please | want |
| bought | hear | pretty | was |
| boy | her | read | went |
| buy | here | really | were |
| can | him | right | when |
| came | his | said | where |
| children | house | saw | white |
| color | into | scared | with |
| come | know | school | would |
| cousin | like | sent | write |
| didn't | little | some | writing |
| does | made | store | wrote |
| don't | make | swimming | your |
| every | many | teacher | you're |

# spelling table

| Sound | Spellings | Examples |
|---|---|---|
| /ă/ | a a_e ai au | ask, have, plaid, laugh |
| /ā/ | a a_e ai ay ea eigh ey | table, save, rain, gray, break, eight, they |
| /ä/ | a ea | father, heart |
| /âr/ | air are ere | chair, care, where |
| /b/ | b bb | best, rabbit |
| /ch/ | ch tch | child, catch |
| /d/ | d dd | dish, add |
| /ĕ/ | e ea ie ue a ai ay | best, read, friend, guess, many, said, says |
| /ē/ | e e_e ea ee ei eo ey y | even, these, each, meet, receive, people, key, city |
| /f/ | f ff gh | fly, off, laugh |
| /g/ | g gg | go, egg |
| /h/ | h wh | hot, who |
| /ĭ/ | i ui e ee u a | inside, build, pretty, been, busy, luggage |
| /ī/ | i i_e ie igh eye uy y | tiny, drive, pie, high, eyes, buy, fly |
| /îr/ | ear eer eir ere | year, deer, weird, here |
| /j/ | j g | jog, danger |
| /k/ | k c ck ch | keep, coat, kick, school |
| /ks/ | x | six |
| /kw/ | qu | quiet |
| /l/ | l ll | late, tell |
| /m/ | m mb mm | much, comb, hammer |
| /n/ | n kn nn | need, know, beginning |
| /ng/ | n ng | thank, bring |

| Sound | Spellings | Examples |
|---|---|---|
| /ŏ/ | o a | shop, was |
| /ō/ | o o_e oa oe ou ow | both, hole, road, toe, boulder, slow |
| /oi/ | oi oy | point, enjoy |
| /ô/ | o oa oo ou ough a au aw | off, coarse, door, four, brought, tall, autumn, draw |
| /o͝o/ | oo ou u u_e | book, could, pull, sure |
| /o͞o/ | oo ou u_e ue ew o | noon, you, June, blue, news, two |
| /ou/ | ou ow | about, owl |
| /p/ | p pp | place, dropped |
| /r/ | r rr wr | rain, sorry, write |
| /s/ | s ss c | safe, dress, city |
| /sh/ | sh s | shook, sure |
| /t/ | t tt ed | take, matter, thanked |
| /th/ | th | then |
| /th/ | th | third |
| /ŭ/ | u o oe | such, mother, does |
| /ûr/ | ur ir er or ear ere our | curl, girl, dessert, world, learn, were, flourish |
| /v/ | v f | even, of |
| /w/ | w wh o | walk, when, one |
| /y/ | y | year |
| /yo͞o/ | u_e ew ue | use, few, Tuesday |
| /z/ | z zz s | sneeze, blizzard, says |
| /ə/ | a e i o u | along, misery, estimate, lion, subtract |

# Answer Key

**Page 8**
1. ask, matter, black, add, match, Saturday, class, apple, subtract, thank, catch, January, after, hammer, half
2. laugh

**Page 9**
1. add
2. matter
3. match
4. class
5. after
6. thank
7. half
8. ask
9. apple
10. subtract
11. hammer
12. black
13. laugh
14. January
15. catch

**Page 10**
Spell correctly: January, catch, apple, after, half
Capitalize: Did, To, You
Add period after: January, glass

**Page 11**
1. hammer, January, matter
2. add, class, match
3. ask, Saturday, thank
4. black, laugh, subtract

**Page 12**
1. page, change, face, save, ate, place, late, safe, came
2. gray, away, pay, May
3. great, break
4. April

**Page 13**
1. came
2. safe
3. away
4. place
5. page
6. great
7. change
8. gray
9. May
10. ate
11. break
12. pay
13. late
14. save
15. face

**Page 14**
Spell correctly: safe, place, away, late, break
Capitalize: It, Dig, Then
Take out: from, to

**Page 15**
Insert words: save, away, gray, May, page, face, great
Capitalize: Heather, Last, Then, He
Add period after: stamps, book, Scooter

**Page 16**
1. rain, sail, afraid, aid, train, wait, aim, paint

**Page 17**
1. aid
2. afraid
3. wait
4. danger
5. able
6. table
7. eight
8. train
9. sail
10. fable
11. rain
12. they
13. weigh
14. paint
15. aim

**Page 18**
Spell correctly: able, train, eight, They, wait
Capitalize: Sanchez, Each, Our
Take out: with, that

**Page 19**
1. cable
2. carton
3. coarse
4. black
5. block
6. scheme
7. comb
8. subtract
9. clock
10. card
11. corn
12. socks

**Page 20**
1. next, egg, end, help, spent, second, forget, dress, address, test
2. ready, read, head
3. again, said
4. says

**Page 21**
1. address
2. again
3. read
4. forget
5. spent
6. ready
7. help
8. says
9. second
10. test
11. said
12. next
13. end
14. dress
15. egg

**Page 22**
Spell correctly: forget, says, head, help, second
Capitalize: I, She
Add period after: things, help, finger

**Page 23**
1. then
2. 3
3. address [page number and number of meanings will vary by dictionary]

**Page 24**
1. tests, pages, papers, hammers, tables, clowns, paints, apples, eggs, hands, trains, places
2. dresses, classes, matches, addresses

**Page 25**
1. paints
2. hammers
3. apples
4. eggs
5. papers
6. pages
7. dresses
8. addresses
9. tests
10. matches
11. trains
12. hands
13. places
14. clowns
15. classes

**Page 26**
Spell correctly: *Pages*, clowns, places, eggs, tables
Capitalize: It, They, You
Add period after: world, movie

**Page 27**
1. addresses, address [number of word forms will vary by dictionary]
2. hands, hand [number of word forms will vary]
3. pages, page [number of word forms will vary]
4. paints, paint [number of word forms will vary]
5. trains, train [number of word forms will vary]

**Page 28**
1. catch
2. half
3. laugh
4. subtract
5. January
6. April
7. place
8. great
9. gray
10. break
11. danger
12. afraid

**Page 29**
13. they
14. weigh
15. table
16. ready
17. again
18. says
19. second
20. address
21. apples
22. eggs
23. hammers
24. places
25. matches

**Page 30**
1. slept, February, them, never, when, sent, kept, September, best, then, cents, Wednesday, better
2. friend
3. many
4. guess

**Page 31**
1. many
2. friend
3. September
4. Wednesday
5. slept
6. February
7. best
8. sent
9. when
10. then
11. kept
12. them
13. better
14. guess
15. never

**Page 32**
Spell correctly: friend, them, guess, kept, September
Capitalize: February, Texas, Kim
Add question mark after: did, September

**Page 33**
1. The book I like best was written by Fred Gibson.
2. It is about a dog called Old Yeller.
3. Travis and Old Yeller have many adventures.
4. Carl Anderson wrote about a horse named Blaze.
5. Blaze was kept by a boy named Billy.
6. A horse named Thunderbolt became friends with Billy and Blaze.

**Page 34**
1. street, free, wheel, queen, sneeze, meet, need, sleep
2. please, read, each, team, sea, dream, meat
3. people

**Page 35**
1. sleep
2. street
3. people
4. sneeze
5. read
6. wheel
7. sea
8. meat
9. team
10. dream
11. meet

**Page 36**
Spell correctly: team, people, meet, each, Read
Capitalize: One, Each, After
Take out: a, of

**Page 37**
1. I had a wonderful dream last night.
2. All the people who live on my street were in it.
3. I used a big wheel to steer our big ship out to sea.
4. We had a feast of fruit and roasted meat on an island.

**Page 38**
1. even
2. only, story, family, sleepy, carry, sunny, funny, very, every, city, penny, happy, busy
3. these
4. key

**Page 39**
1. carry
2. very
3. key
4. funny
5. every
6. penny
7. these
8. story
9. only
10. happy
11. sunny
12. busy
13. city
14. sleepy
15. even

**Page 40**
Spell correctly: city, family, happy, busy, very
Capitalize: She, We, Thursday
Add period after: Illinois, morning

**Page 41**
1-3. [page numbers will vary by dictionary]
4. carry [page number will vary]
5. even [page number will vary]
6. funny [page number will vary]
7. key [page number will vary]

**Page 42**
1. Sunday, under, summer, sun, lunch, such, much
2. does
3. from, money, nothing, mother, month, front, other, Monday

**Page 43**
1. front
2. under
3. money
4. such
5. nothing
6. does
7. month
8. Monday
9. from
10. sun
11. Sunday
12. mother
13. much
14. summer
15. other

**Page 44**
Spell correctly: money, Monday, Summer, front, lunch
Capitalize: Each, Sunday, Does
Add question mark after: it, you

**Page 45**
1. What comes once in a month, twice in a moment, but never in a hundred years? the letter _m_
2. What do you lose whenever you stand up? your lap
3. What can you put into the apple pie you have for lunch? your teeth

**Page 46**
1. they'll, you'll, I'll, we'll, she'll
2. I've, we've, you've, they've
3. I'd, you'd, they'd
4. she's, it's, he's
5. I'm

**Page 47**
1. It's
2. I've
3. He's
4. You'll
5. You've
6. They'd
7. They've
8. We'll
9. We've
10. I'm
11. She's
12. they'll
13. we'll
14. you'd
15. I'll

**Page 48**
Spell correctly: I'm, I'd, We've, I've, We'll
Capitalize: Pete, Collins
Add period after: neighborhood, station, owner

**Page 49**
1. I'll, wi
2. he's, i
3. it's, i
4. they've, ha
5. you'd, ha
6. I'm, a
7. you'd, woul
8. she's, ha

**Page 50**
1. friend
2. Wednesday
3. guess
4. many
5. February
6. queen
7. team
8. people
9. meet
10. please
11. family
12. even
13. every

**Page 51**
14. key
15. these
16. does
17. month
18. other
19. lunch
20. such
21. I'm
22. you've
23. she'll
24. they'd
25. it's

**Page 52**
1. just, hundred, sum, must, butter, supper, number
2. won, cover
3. lovely, something, done, some, shove, none, one

**Page 53**
1. won
2. cover
3. something
4. some
5. sum
6. one
7. hundred
8. must
9. number
10. none
11. done
12. lovely
13. shove
14. just
15. supper

**Page 54**
Spell correctly: just, number, lovely, hundred, done
Capitalize: Yesterday, Rocket, Now
Add period after: soon, state

**Page 55**
1. sail
2. sale
3. ate
4. eight
5. sun
6. son
7. won
8. one
9. sum, some

**Page 56**
1. thing, little, winter, kick, river, dish, fill, think, spring, which, children
2. pretty, December
3. begin
4. build
5. been

**Page 57**
1. kick
2. children
3. build
4. river
5. winter
6. dish
7. begin
8. pretty
9. little
10. think
11. which
12. been
13. spring
14. fill
15. thing

**Page 58**
Spell correctly: build, winter, river, December, spring
Capitalize: Luke, I, Maybe
Add period after: barn, year

**Page 59**
1. little; circle "simple", "little"
2. many; circle "many", "thick"
3. icy; circle "cold", "icy"
4. dangerous; circle "Thin", "some", "dangerous"
5. pretty; circle "Many", "pretty"
6. hot; circle "hot", "summer"
7. shallow; circle "large", "shallow"
8. brown; circle "red", "brown"
9. every; circle "every"

**Page 60**
1. alike, while, white, line, size, miles, times, nice, drive, write, inside, mine, shine
2. lion, tiny
3. eyes

**Page 61**
1. drive
2. miles
3. line
4. while
5. size
6. shine
7. nice
8. mine
9. times
10. white
11. eyes
12. write
13. tiny
14. alike
15. inside

**Page 62**
Spell correctly: miles, line, inside, eyes, tiny
Capitalize: They, Once, Check
Add period after: cheers, disappointed

**Page 63**
1-4. [guide words and page numbers will vary by dictionary]

**Page 64**
1. Friday, kind, child, mind, behind
2. fly, why, try, sky, cry, by

3. high, right, light, night
4. buy

**Page 65**
1. behind
2. fly
3. Friday
4. kind
5. by
6. right
7. light
8. high
9. child
10. cry
11. night
12. try
13. buy
14. mind
15. why

**Page 66**
Spell correctly: Friday, behind, night, mind, why
Capitalize: Sam, That, Write
Add period after: again, sock

**Page 67**
1. second
2. k
3. t
4. sky, story
5. behind, buy, by
6. finish, fly, Friday

**Page 68**
1. wished, asked, dreamed, rained, handed, painted, filled, subtracted, thanked, waited
2. ending, guessing, laughing, meeting, sleeping, reading

**Page 69**
1. handed
2. thanked
3. waited
4. meeting
5. guessing
6. dreamed
7. rained
8. wished
9. painted
10. reading
11. sleeping
12. asked
13. laughing
14. ending
15. filled

**Page 70**
Spell correctly: meeting, thanked, wished, asked, ending
Capitalize: This, He, The
Take out: to, it

**Page 71**
1. Betsy asked Paul, "Who painted this picture?"
2. She saw that Paul was sleeping.
3. Betsy shouted, "Boo!"
4. Paul jumped up fast.
5. "Oh, Betsy," he cried. "Now I'll never know the ending of my dream!"
6. They both started laughing.

**Page 72**
1. lovely
2. hundred
3. won
4. butter
5. done
6. which
7. been
8. pretty
9. build
10. children
11. eyes
12. write
13. lion

**Page 73**
14. while
15. tiny
16. Why
17. buy
18. right
19. night
20. behind
21. laughing
22. wished
23. guessing
24. dreamed
25. thanked

**Page 74**
1. October, shop, block, bottle, o'clock, sorry, socks, problem, jog, clock, bottom, forgot, body
2. what, wash, was

**Page 75**
1. socks
2. block
3. jog
4. sorry
5. what
6. forgot
7. o'clock
8. was
9. October
10. body
11. bottom
12. shop
13. problem
14. wash
15. bottle

**Page 76**
Spell correctly: socks, bottom, jog, block, problem
Capitalize: Today, They, Sparky
Add period after: school, them

**Page 77**
1. cap, children, clock, cover
2. salt, shop, sorry, stack
3. wash, west, what, wonder
4. farmer, feed, forgot, funny

**Page 78**
1. whole, hope, joke, wrote, alone, hole, close
2. slow, blow, show, yellow, snow, know
3. goes, toe
4. November

**Page 79**
1. goes
2. wrote
3. hope
4. whole
5. know
6. alone

7. yellow
8. close
9. November
10. toe
11. snow
12. blow
13. hole
14. slow
15. show

**Page 80**
Spell correctly: November, know, hope, yellow, goes
Capitalize: I, Thanks, Why
Add period after: sweater, tablet

**Page 81**
1. Jack (hurt) his toe.
2. Please (show) me your new shoes.
3. Snow (fell) all night long.
4. We (ate) the whole pizza.
5. Krista (bought) a yellow skateboard
6. Scooter (dug) a hole in the yard.
7. Ming (wrote) a story about a crow.
8. Mrs. Sosa (goes) to lunch with our class.

**Page 82**
1. most, ago, hold, hello, open, over, comb, almost, both, gold
2. coat, loaf, toast, boat, road
3. cocoa

**Page 83**
1. comb
2. gold
3. ago
4. both
5. hello
6. hold
7. most
8. almost
9. open
10. over
11. loaf
12. coat
13. toast
14. road
15. boat

**Page 84**
Spell correctly: Hello, gold, comb, loaf, toast
Capitalize: Adam, We, Do
Add question mark after: beach, jam

**Page 85**
ACROSS
3. both
4. cocoa
6. road
7. hold
DOWN
1. over
2. coat
3. ago
5. almost
6. boat

**Page 86**
1. book, took, cook, stood, wood, poor, foot, shook, cookies
2. sure, put, full, pull
3. should, would, could

**Page 87**
1. pull
2. stood
3. sure
4. poor
5. full
6. took
7. foot
8. should
9. wood
10. cookies
11. could
12. cook
13. put
14. would
15. shook

**Page 88**
Spell correctly: stood, pull, poor, Could, sure
Capitalize: The, What, If
Take out: an, that

**Page 89**
1. Many wood products come from Maine.
2. I am sure that the largest state is Alaska.
3. Everyone should visit Chicago, Illinois.
4. Would you like to go to New Orleans?
5. San Francisco shook during an earthquake.
6. My friend from Toronto sent me some cookies.

**Page 90**
1. sneezed, smiling, hoped, shining, pleased, liked, taking, driving, closed
2. beginning, dropping, stopped, dropped, jogged, hopping, shopping

**Page 91**
1. jogged
2. beginning
3. closed
4. hoped
5. liked
6. shining
7. stopped
8. smiling
9. hopping
10. sneezed
11. taking
12. dropped
13. driving
14. pleased
15. dropping

**Page 92**
Spell correctly: stopped, liked, pleased, smiling, driving
Capitalize: I, My, When
Add period after: one, soon

**Page 93**
1. School closed for vacation on May 28, 2004.
2. On June 25, 1999, Ms. Padden jogged in a race.
3. Old friends dropped in to visit us on February 4, 2003.
4. Ana hoped her party would be on May 17, 2006.

**Page 94**
1. o'clock
2. bottle
3. socks
4. wash
5. hole
6. yellow
7. wrote
8. goes
9. know
10. November
11. toast
12. almost

**Page 95**
13. comb
14. road
15. hello
16. cookies
17. poor
18. should
19. shook
20. sure
21. shining
22. dropped
23. hoped
24. stopped
25. hopping

**Page 96**
1. noon, tooth, school, too
2. blue, Tuesday, true, few, knew, news
3. huge, used, June
4. who, two, move

**Page 97**
1. noon
2. news
3. who
4. tooth
5. move
6. school
7. blue
8. June
9. few
10. two
11. too
12. huge
13. true
14. used
15. knew

**Page 98**
Spell correctly: Tuesday, noon, two, blue, who
Capitalize: Here, It, Guess
Add period after: track, race

**Page 99**
1. few
2. tooth
3. move
4. huge

**Page 100**
1. curl, turn, Thursday, fur
2. girl, bird, first, dirt, third
3. world, word, work, worm
4. learn, earth
5. were

**Page 101**
1. worm
2. girl
3. earth or Earth
4. first
5. third
6. turn
7. Thursday

8. word
9. dirt
10. were
11. learn
12. work
13. curl
14. world
15. fur

**Page 102**
Spell correctly: worm, third, curl, dirt, earth
Capitalize: The, He, The
Add period after: it, morning

**Page 103**
1. add
2. dirty
3. huge
4. young
5. full, empty
6. turn, spin
7. first, last
8. earth, world

**Page 104**
1. dark, yard, art, market, garden, hard, father, March, arm, barn, start, star, card, sharp, bark
2. heart

**Page 105**
1. garden
2. market
3. March
4. card
5. barn
6. yard
7. dark
8. hard
9. father
10. sharp
11. start
12. art
13. star, star
14. heart, heart
15. bark, bark

**Page 106**
Spell correctly: card, art, start, garden, yard
Capitalize: Are, We, Mary
Add question mark after: sing, us

**Page 107**
1. Meaning 2
2. Meaning 1 [sentences will vary]

**Page 108**
1. coin, choice, spoil, boil, voice, soil, noise, point, broil, join, oil
2. boy, royal, toy, joy, enjoy

**Page 109**
1. royal
2. oil
3. toy
4. joy
5. voice
6. spoil
7. join
8. coin
9. boy
10. enjoy
11. choice
12. noise
13. soil
14. broil
15. point

**Page 110**
Spell correctly: royal, choice, spoil, joy, voice
Capitalize: Nothing, James, Send
Add period after: want, joy

**Page 111**
1. We will (enjoy) visiting Minneapolis.
2. My dog Max makes a lot of (noise)!
3. Can you (point) out Mallory Street?
4. This (coin) was made in Colorado.
5. Mrs. Hays bought a (toy) for her baby.
6. Kevin and I want to (join) the baseball team.

**Page 112**
1. isn't, weren't, doesn't, hadn't, mustn't, wouldn't, won't, shouldn't, aren't, wasn't, don't, couldn't, didn't, hasn't, haven't
2. can't

**Page 113**
1. won't
2. don't
3. couldn't
4. wouldn't
5. doesn't
6. wasn't
7. hadn't
8. mustn't
9. didn't
10. can't
11. hasn't
12. haven't
13. aren't
14. weren't
15. isn't

**Page 114**
Spell correctly: couldn't, hasn't, Wouldn't, won't, Doesn't
Capitalize: It, Rose, You
Take out: in, like

**Page 115**
1. isn't
2. aren't
3. weren't
4. wasn't

**Page 116**
1. true
2. used
3. too
4. Two
5. knew
6. Few
7. huge
8. girl
9. were
10. curl
11. earth
12. worm

**Page 117**
13. sharp
14. father
15. garden
16. heart
17. voice
18. enjoy
19. royal
20. soil
21. can't
22. aren't

23. haven't
24. won't
25. weren't

**Page 118**
1. frog, along, long, off, belong, strong
2. walk, water, always, mall, tall, talk
3. bought, brought
4. because
5. draw

**Page 119**
1. tall
2. off
3. always
4. strong
5. long
6. talk
7. water
8. mall
9. brought
10. draw
11. frog
12. belong
13. along
14. walk
15. bought

**Page 120**
Spell correctly: always, talk, water, because, along
Capitalize: Jane, I, It's, We
Take out: you, me

**Page 121**
1. My (sister) hid behind a tall tree.
2. (Ling) bought a baseball.
3. (Mrs. Martinez) took a long vacation.
4. (I) will draw a picture of you.
5. (The old clock) fell off the shelf.

**Page 122**
1. August, autumn
2. morning, popcorn, before, corner, storm, north, born, fork, sport
3. door, floor, four, pour
4. quart

**Page 123**
1. popcorn
2. fork
3. storm
4. corner
5. pour
6. north
7. autumn
8. morning
9. before
10. quart
11. floor
12. door
13. four
14. sport
15. born

**Page 124**
Spell correctly: sport, Before, popcorn, storm, morning
Capitalize: Here, Also, You
Add period after: go, backpack

**Page 125**
1. August, aunt, autumn
2. point, porch, pour
3. foggy, fond, four
4. money, moon, morning

**Page 126**
1. house, sound, ground, found, about, hour, around, count, our
2. flower, town, tower, brown, power, down, owl

**Page 127**
1. house
2. sound
3. hour
4. tower
5. owl
6. down
7. power
8. about
9. flower
10. ground
11. found
12. count
13. brown
14. around
15. our

**Page 128**
Spell correctly: sound, house, owl, brown, about
Capitalize: We, It, Chris
Take out: our, to

**Page 129**
1. broth
2. maintain
3. admire
4. dome
5. fire
6. wire
7. starch
8. deer, dear

**Page 130**
1. n(ear), h(ear), d(eer), e(ar), y(ear), h(ere), d(ear)
2. c(are), wh(ere), st(air)s, ch(air), a(ir), h(air)
3. f(ire), w(ire), t(ire)

**Page 131**
1. hair
2. stairs
3. wire
4. dear
5. air
6. deer
7. hear
8. care
9. ear
10. year
11. near
12. where
13. tire
14. fire
15. here

**Page 132**
Spell correctly: chair, near, air, care, year
Capitalize: Are, Do, I
Add question mark after: nights, read

**Page 133**
1. stairs, where, hair
2. fire, wire, tire
3. year, here, near

**Page 134**
1. taller, tallest, longer, longest, stronger, strongest, greater, greatest, sharper, sharpest
2. dirtier, dirtiest, funnier, funniest
3. hotter, hottest

**Page 135**
1. hotter
2. sharpest
3. sharper
4. strongest
5. dirtiest
6. taller
7. funniest
8. tallest
9. greater
10. longer
11. stronger
12. longest
13. hottest
14. greatest
15. funnier

**Page 136**
Spell correctly: greatest, longer, taller, dirtier, greater
Capitalize: Spring, The, Having
Add period after: all, garden

**Page 137**
1. Sharon tells the funniest jokes we've ever heard.
2. The sun is hotter today than it was yesterday.
3. Gigi is the tallest girl on the basketball team.
4. Twenty is greater than ten.

**Page 138**
1. bought
2. because
3. strong
4. talk
5. draw
6. quart
7. pour
8. autumn
9. before
10. floor

**Page 139**
11. hour
12. owl
13. count
14. tower
15. air
16. deer
17. where
18. here
19. wire
20. near
21. care
22. sharpest
23. greater
24. hottest
25. funnier